SRA
Reading
Mastery®
Transformations

Reading
Workbook

Siegfried Engelmann

Steve Osborn

Jean Osborn

Leslie Zoref

Mc
Graw
Hill

Acknowledgments

Many thanks to Lynda Gansel and Crystal Weber for their
help in preparing the manuscript.

mheducation.com/prek-12

Send all inquiries to:
McGraw-Hill Education
8787 Orion Place
Columbus, OH 43240

ISBN: 978-0-07-905377-0
MHID: 0-07-905377-7

Printed in the United States of America.

1 2 3 4 5 6 7 8 9 QSX 25 24 23 22 21 20

A STORY DETAILS

Work the items.

1. What is the title of the story?

   _____

2. Who is the main character in the story?

   _____

3. In what state does Ron live?

   _____

4. Which room was Ron sitting in at the beginning of the story?

   a. Ms. Green's fourth-grade classroom

   b. Ms. Brown's third-grade classroom

   c. Ms. Brown's fourth-grade classroom

5. Ron saw ▮▮▮ posters on the wall.

   a. travel   b. movie   c. fashion

6. When Ron saw the posters, he began dreaming about ▮▮▮ .

   a. playing baseball   b. a real vacation

   c. watching TV

7. What hadn't Ron's family done for six years?

   a. bought a new car

   b. built an extra bedroom

   c. taken a vacation

8. Debby was Ron's ▮▮▮ .

   a. sister   b. mother   c. girlfriend

9. What was Debby's idea of fun?

   a. drawing pictures   b. going to dances

   c. playing video games

B VOCABULARY FROM CONTEXT

Complete each sentence with the correct word.

1. Because it was a _____ day, nobody was at school.

   • school   • work   • vacation

2. The artist made a drawing in her

   _____ .

   • sketchbook   • pencil   • workbook

3. The man paddled down the river in a

   _____ .

   • car   • kayak   • powerboat

4. We decided to eat bananas

   _____ of grapes.

   • instead   • because   • made

5. The _____ advertised the beach club.

   • sand   • ocean   • poster

6. The teacher's homework

   _____ was quite difficult.

   • discussion • assignment • assessment

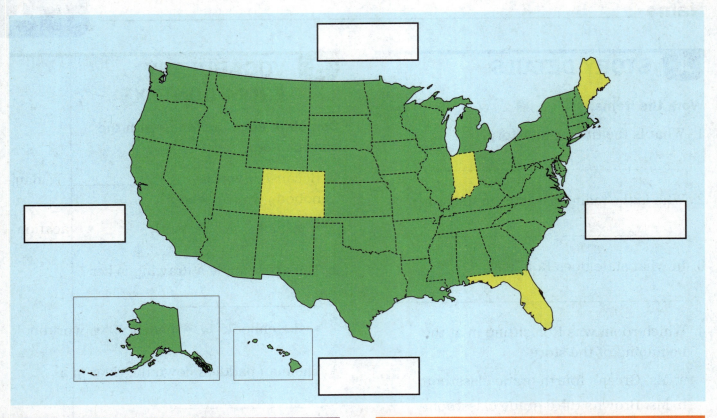

C MAPS

The map above shows the United States. The boxes around the map show the four directions. Here are the rules about map directions:

- North is at the top.
- South is at the bottom.
- East is on the right side.
- West is on the left side.

1. Write the correct directions in the boxes around the map.

2. Label the four yellow states as follows:
   - Write **I** on Indiana.
   - Write **C** on Colorado.
   - Write **M** on Maine.
   - Write **F** on Florida.

D SEQUENCING

Number the events in the correct sequence.

_____ The school bell rang.

_____ Ron looked at posters on the wall.

_____ Ms. Brown gave a homework assignment.

GO TO PART C IN YOUR TEXTBOOK

Name ______________________________

A STORY DETAILS

Work the items.

1. For his homework assignment, Ron had to write about ____ .
   a. his summer vacation
   b. his trip to Maine   c. Flatville, Indiana

2. Ron's mom didn't pick him up from school because she ____ .
   a. was on vacation   b. had a flat tire
   c. had to work until 6

3. Ron decided to go home by ____ .
   a. riding the bus   b. walking
   c. riding his bike

4. Ron decided to use the ____ in the library.
   a. video game   b. computer
   c. vending machine

5. What did Ron plan to do with that device?
   a. buy candy   b. play a game
   c. write a story

6. Ron called Debby to tell her he ____ .
   a. would be late
   b. had finished his story
   c. was bored

7. Ron wrote, "I spent my summer in one of the hottest ____ in America.
   a. vacation spots
   b. deserts
   c. small towns

8. Ron closed his eyes when he was writing so he could ____ .
   a. go to sleep
   b. get a picture in his mind   c. rub them

9. When Ron opened his eyes again, he thought he was in ____ .
   a. Maine   b. Indiana   c. Florida

B VOCABULARY FROM CONTEXT

Complete each sentence with the correct word.

1. The ________________ at the grocery store took money and made change.
   • customers   • food   • cashier

2. Because the cat had ________________, nobody could find her.
   • vanished   • appeared   • slept

3. The ________________ starting time for school is eight-thirty in the morning.
   • usual   • jump   • afternoon

4. In the ________________, the water moved quickly and sprayed into the air.
   • pond   • rapids   • bathtub

5. The birds were ________________ by the loud noise.
   • expected   • produced   • startled

6. The boy was ________________ several presents for his birthday.
   • expecting   • giving away   • buying

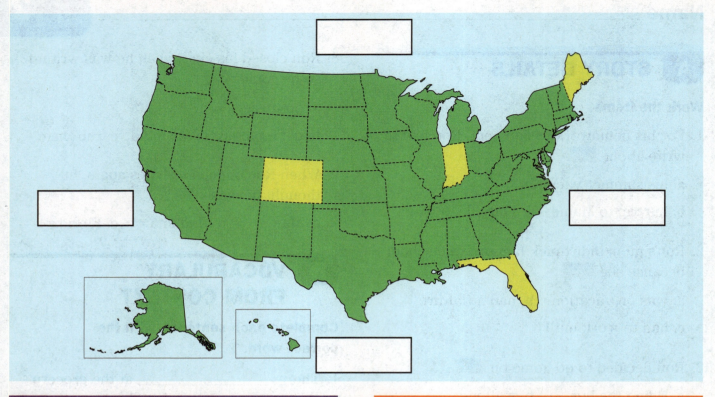

C   MAPS

The map shows the United States.

1. Write the correct directions in the boxes around the map.

2. Label the four yellow states as follows:
   - Write **I** on Indiana.
   - Write **C** on Colorado.
   - Write **M** on Maine.
   - Write **F** on Florida.

3. Which labeled state is the farthest south on the map?

   _____

4. Which labeled state is the farthest north on the map?

   _____

D   SEQUENCING

Number the events in the correct sequence.

_____ Ron decided to walk home.

_____ Ron wrote about his summer vacation.

_____ Ron entered the library.

GO TO PART C IN YOUR TEXTBOOK

A STORY DETAILS

Work the items.

1. Which state does Ron live in?

   _____

2. Which state is Ron visiting in Chapter 3?

   _____

3. What type of boat is Ron riding in?

   _____

4. To make the boat turn left, Ron paddled on the ▢ .

   a. left side   b. right side   c. inside

5. To make the boat turn right, Ron paddled on the ▢ .

   a. left side   b. right side   c. inside

6. To make the boat go straight, Ron made ▢ numbers of left and right strokes.

   a. odd   b. equal   c. unequal

7. After the bend in the river, the water moved ▢ .

   a. the same   b. slower   c. faster

8. The person who yelled at Ron was his ▢ .

   a. teacher   b. mother   c. sister

9. That person wanted Ron to ▢ the river.

   a. get out of   b. stay in   c. go back up

B VOCABULARY FROM CONTEXT

Complete each sentence with the correct word.

1. Because he _____ money, the man couldn't buy a car.

   • liked   • made   • lacked

2. The students studied _____ and other types of rocks.

   • boulders   • baldness   • builders

3. When she _____ the rain, the woman took out her umbrella.

   • buried   • stopped   • noticed

4. The backpack was filled with food and other _____ .

   • bricks   • supplies   • support

5. The girl _____ her shoulders to show she didn't care.

   • sunburned   • shrugged   • shaved

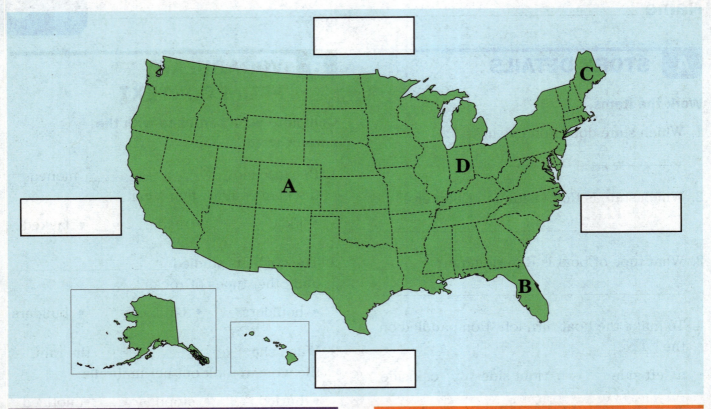

C MAPS

Work the items.

1. Write the correct directions in the boxes around the map.

2. What is the name of state A on the map?

   _____

3. What is the name of state B on the map?

   _____

4. Write the name of the state that Ron is visiting.

   _____

5. Write the name of the state that Ron lives in.

   _____

D SEQUENCING

Number the events in the correct sequence.

_____ Ron headed into the rapids.

_____ Ron sat in Ms. Brown's classroom.

_____ Ron paddled a kayak in calm water.

GO TO PART E IN YOUR TEXTBOOK

A STORY DETAILS

Work the items.

1. The first boulder was ▨ the river.

   a. beside   b. in the middle of   c. next to

2. ▨ of the river flowed around the right side of the boulder.

   a. One third   b. Half   c. Two thirds

3. After Ron passed the boulder, he ▨ .

   a. turned left   b. turned right

   c. went with the current

4. The second boulder was located on the edge of a ▨ .

   a. pool   b. waterfall   c. rapids

5. When the kayak hit the second boulder, it ▨ .

   a. sank to the bottom   b. split in two

   c. flipped up in the air

6. Ron landed ▨ after he left the kayak.

   a. in the pool   b. on shore

   c. on top of the boulder

7. Ron took off his shoes and shirt because they were ▨ .

   a. bloody   b. torn   c. wet

8. Ron figured that his ▨ would come looking for him.

   a. mother   b. brother   c. sister

9. Ron used his ▨ as a pillow.

   a. life jacket   b. shirt   c. shoes

B VOCABULARY FROM CONTEXT

Complete each sentence with the correct word.

1. The cat _____ the bird very quietly and slowly.

   • ignored   • meowed at   • approached

2. Because the _____ was so swift, no one could swim in the river.

   • current   • boat   • fish

3. Climbing steep cliffs is a very

   _____ sport.

   • easy   • dangerous   • safe

4. It was hard to _____ the loud siren on the fire engine.

   • ignore   • hear   • pay attention to

5. The magician said he could make the

   rabbit _____ without a trace.

   • hop   • shiver   • disappear

C SEQUENCING

Number the events in the correct sequence.

_____ Ron's kayak hit a boulder straight on.

_____ Ron fell asleep.

_____ Ron passed a boulder on the left side.

_____ Ron fell into a pool of water.

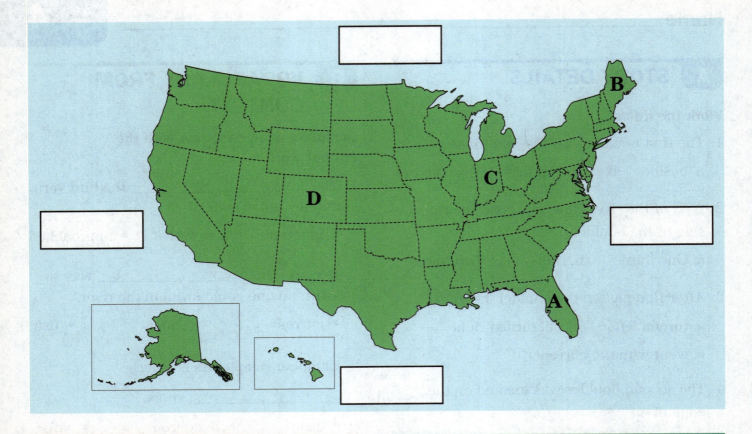

D MAPS

Work the items.

1. Write the correct directions in the boxes around the map.

2. What is the name of state A on the map?

   _____

3. What is the name of state B on the map?

   _____

4. Which lettered state on the map is the farthest west?

   _____

5. Which lettered state on the map is the farthest south?

   _____

E REFERRING TO TEXT

In the paragraph below, underline the sentence that tells what Ron hoped would happen when he smashed into the boulder.

Meanwhile, the edge of the waterfall came closer and closer. As Ron approached, he saw a boulder sticking just a few feet out of the water right at the edge of the waterfall. His only chance was to smash the kayak against the boulder and hope that it would stop him from going over. Besides, the current was taking him straight toward the boulder, so he had no other choice.

GO TO PART D IN YOUR TEXTBOOK

A STORY DETAILS

Work the items.

1. When Ron stood up, Debby gave him a ▓▓▓ .

   a. slap across the face   b. big hug

   c. long, cold stare

2. The man from the kayak shed was named

   Mr. _____ .

3. Ron's kayak was ▓▓▓ .

   a. lost   b. not damaged   c. smashed

4. Debby said they'd been in Maine for three

   _____ .

5. Ron thought they'd been in Maine for a few

   _____ .

6. To pay for the kayak, Debby gave
   Mr. Mason ▓▓▓ .

   a. one hundred dollars   b. a picture

   c. a check

7. Ron had seen that picture before in ▓▓▓ .

   a. the library   b. Debby's room

   c. his classroom

8. When Ron reached for the picture, his
   fingers touched ▓▓▓ .

   a. paper   b. water   c. glass

9. According to Ron's new story, one of the
   hottest vacation spots in America is the

   _____ .

B VOCABULARY FROM CONTEXT

Complete each sentence with the correct word.

1. You need to say "Thank you" when you

   _____ a gift.

   • expect   • reject   • accept

2. You can _____ the same
   color eyes as your parents.

   • inherit   • demerit   • ferret

3. Your brother or sister is your

   _____ .

   • parent   • ancestor   • sibling

4. The friendly coach treated every player

   with _____ .

   • respect   • contempt   • reject

5. None of the goats could beat the

   _____ goat in a fight.

   • sleeping   • dominant   • weakest

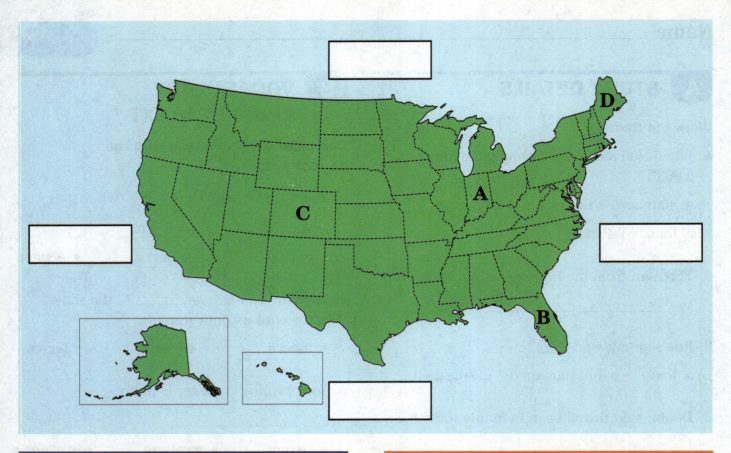

C MAPS

Work the items.

1. Write the correct directions in the boxes around the map.

2. What is the name of state A on the map?

   _____

3. What is the name of state B on the map?

   _____

4. What is the name of state C on the map?

   _____

5. What is the name of the state that Ron visited in his dream?

   _____

D CHARACTER TRAITS

Complete each sentence with *Ron, Debby, Mr. Mason*, or *Ron's mom*.

1. _____ disobeyed his sister.

2. _____ drew pictures in a sketchbook.

3. _____ got a better job.

4. _____ dreamed about a vacation.

5. _____ worked as a cashier.

GO TO PART C IN YOUR TEXTBOOK

Name _____

6

A   STORY DETAILS

Work the items.

1. Your dog wants to be the ▓▓ of you.

   a. servant   b. equal   c. boss

2. Dogs try to establish their ▓▓ within a group.

   a. rank   b. tails   c. barks

3. The leaders in a wolf pack are called the ▓▓ pair.

   a. beta   b. kappa   c. alpha

4. Dogs use ▓▓ language to show who's in charge.

   a. human   b. body   c. foul

5. A dog shows its ▓▓ by making itself look bigger.

   a. fear   b. dominance

   c. love

6. Blinking shows that a lower-ranking dog wants to ▓▓ .

   a. keep the peace   b. start a fight

   c. cry

7. Dominant dogs avoid conflict by ▓▓ .

   a. hiding their tails

   b. going to sleep

   c. scratching themselves

8. Puppies ask for food by ▓▓ an adult dog's face.

   a. biting   b. barking into

   c. licking

9. An alpha dog can become ▓▓ when it feels responsible for a pack of humans.

   a. sleepy   b. stressed

   c. peaceful

B   VOCABULARY

Complete each sentence with the correct word.

acknowledge	ancestor	express
aggressive	behavior	intention

1. The way you act is your

   _____ .

2. You _____ feelings and ideas by what you do or say.

3. A person in your family who lived before your grandparents is your

   _____ .

4. When you agree that something is true, you _____ that it is true.

5. Something you plan to do is your

   _____ .

Copyright © McGraw-Hill Education

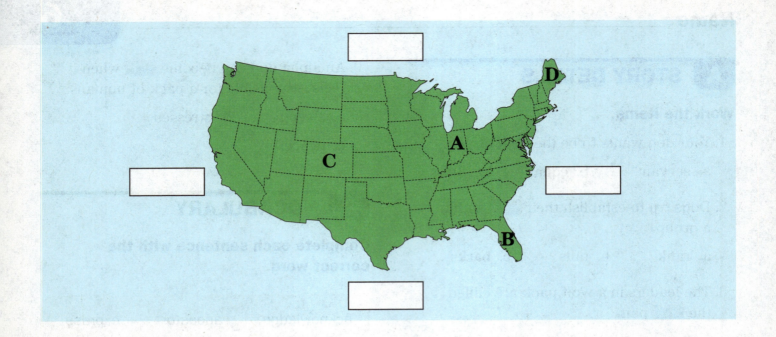

C MAPS

Work the items.

1. Write the correct directions in the boxes around the map.

2. The map shows four lettered states. What is the name of the lettered state that is the farthest west on the map?

   _____

3. What is the name of the lettered state that is the farthest north on the map?

   _____

4. What is the name of the lettered state that is the farthest south on the map?

   _____

5. What is the name of the lettered state that is in between the other lettered states?

   _____

D VOCABULARY FROM CONTEXT

Circle the letter of the choice that means the same thing as the boldface word or phrase.

1. To be sure, dogs do show **affection** to humans. But some of their behaviors have more to do with power than love.

   a. effect   b. hatred   c. love

2. One way a dog shows **dominance** is by making itself look bigger.

   a. shyness   b. power over others

   c. friendliness

3. Puppies learn about **social interaction** through play. They explore how to get along in their pack. They learn which behaviors are acceptable and which are not.

   a. hunting other animals

   b. getting along with each other

   c. commands from people

GO TO PART D IN YOUR TEXTBOOK

A STORY DETAILS

Work the items.

1. What was Gorilla's real name?

   a. George   b. Gabby   c. Gus

2. Bob said that Gorilla would ▓▓▓ in a minute if Walter stood up to him.

   a. crumble   b. crush Walter

   c. sneer

3. Where was Walter's customary seat in the cafeteria?

   a. next to Bob

   b. at a crowded table

   c. at an empty table

4. Bob gave Walter a card for ▓▓▓ Clothing Shop.

   a. Gucci's   b. Calducci's

   c. Calzone's

5. The back of Walter's jacket said

   _____ of the Mountain.

6. Walter's skin ▓▓▓ when he put on the jacket.

   a. tangled   b. tingled

   c. tumbled

7. The owner of the shop agreed to ▓▓▓ the jacket to Walter.

   a. loan   b. sell   c. give

8. Walter scored _____ points on the surprise quiz.

9. Walter told Gorilla to climb a tree and leave the jungle floor to ▓▓▓ humans.

   a. stronger   b. smaller

   c. intelligent

B VOCABULARY

Complete each sentence with the correct word.

arouse	customary	fret
bewildered	flustered	sneer

1. The driver began to _____ after she took a wrong turn.

2. The big brother liked to

   _____ when he spoke to his younger sister.

3. It is _____ for school to begin in the early morning.

4. It was hard to _____ the sleepy student with an alarm clock.

5. When you are confused and nervous,

   you are _____ .

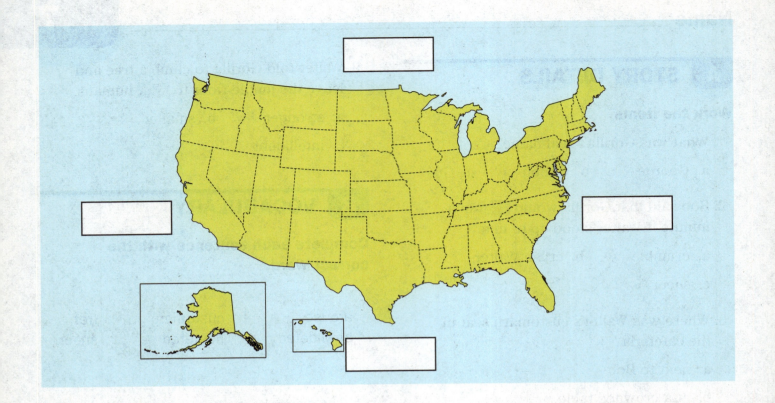

C MAPS

Work the items

1. Write the correct directions in the boxes around the map.

2. Write **C** on Colorado.

3. Write **F** on Florida.

4. Write **I** on Indiana.

5. Write **M** on Maine.

D REFERRING TO TEXT

In the paragraph below, underline the sentence that tells why kids don't call Gus his nickname to his face.

It all started one Friday during lunch period. I was standing in line in the school cafeteria when "Gorilla" Gordon walked up to me. His real name is Gus, but everyone calls him Gorilla because he looks and acts like one. Of course, most kids only call him that behind his back. You live longer that way.

GO TO PART E IN YOUR TEXTBOOK

A STORY DETAILS

Work the items.

1. Walter was a ▮▮▮ for class president.

   a. predicate   b. syndicate

   c. candidate

2. Just before giving his speech, Walter was ▮▮▮ .

   a. in the audience

   b. at the front of the stage

   c. backstage

3. Why did Walter take off his jacket before his speech?

   a. He didn't want to wear it any more.

   b. He couldn't lift the podium while wearing the jacket.

   c. The stage was too hot for wearing a jacket.

4. Why did Walter think Gorilla had taken the jacket?

   a. Gorilla wanted to wear it himself.

   b. Gorilla wanted to take revenge on Walter.

   c. Gorilla saw that the jacket needed to be repaired.

5. Walter tried to ▮▮▮ about losing the jacket.

   a. be philosophical

   b. sound an alarm

   c. get mad

6. Walter said that all anyone needs is a little ▮▮▮ to scale the mountain.

   a. conference   b. consequence

   c. confidence

7. After Walter's speech, some kids gave him a standing ▮▮▮ .

   a. ovation   b. oration

   c. notation

8. Mr. Calducci said that all his clothes were on short-term _____ .

9. Why didn't Walter need the jacket at the end of the story?

   a. It was too small for him.

   b. He couldn't afford it.

   c. He had realized his potential.

B VOCABULARY

Complete each sentence with the correct word.

candidate	ovation	potential
expectant	philosophical	
improvise	podium	

1. The audience gave the actors a standing _____ when the play was over.

2. You couldn't see the speaker's legs because she was standing behind the

   _____ .

3. The winning _____ is the one who gets the most votes.

4. Walter felt that everyone has the _____ to succeed.

5. Kama had a really _____ look on her face when she started to open the gift.

6. Some musicians _____ instead of playing from a score.

C REFERRING TO TEXT

1. Underline the sentence that tells how Walter felt about his speech.

The day before the election was to be held, each candidate was supposed to give a short speech in a special assembly. I wrote my speech the night before. (It was brilliant, of course!) When I finished, I folded the speech and put it in my jacket pocket.

2. Underline the sentence that tells why Walter took off his jacket.

Ms. Bateman asked me if I'd carry the wooden speaker's podium from backstage to center stage. It must have weighed fifty tons, and it was tough trying to lift it with my jacket on. So I took off the jacket and carefully folded it over a chair backstage. Then I lugged the podium out to the middle of the stage as the students took their seats in the auditorium.

D VOCABULARY FROM CONTEXT

Circle the letter of the choice that means the same thing as the boldface word.

1. The shoe company used ads to **arouse** interest in their sandals.

   a. decrease   b. awaken

   c. eliminate

2. Karan began to **fret** about his lost hat.

   a. worry   b. feel calm

   c. scratch

3. The big, mean boxer **sneered at** his small, weak opponent.

   a. sneezed at   b. mocked

   c. acted friendly to

4. It is **customary** to have salt and pepper shakers on the dinner table.

   a. usual   b. unusual

   c. costumed

5. The American tourist was **bewildered** by the signs in Chinese.

   a. made wild   b. comforted

   c. confused

GO TO PART C IN YOUR TEXTBOOK

A STORY DETAILS

Work the items.

1. The title of the novel you are reading is

   the _____ Wizard of Oz.

2. The author of the novel is L. Frank

   _____ .

3. What state does the first chapter of the novel tell about?

   _____

4. Dorothy lived with Aunt

   _____ and Uncle

   _____ .

5. The name of Dorothy's dog was

   _____ .

6. Dorothy's aunt was ▒▒ by the sound of Dorothy's laughter.

   a. cheered up   b. startled

   c. pleased

7. Dorothy's uncle had a ▒▒ expression on his face.

   a. stern   b. happy

   c. timid

8. A cyclone cellar was ▒▒ Dorothy's house.

   a. next to   b. under

   c. above

9. Dorothy's family used that cellar to hide from ▒▒ .

   a. whirlwinds   b. tidal waves

   c. fires

B CHARACTER TRAITS

Complete each sentence with *Dorothy, Toto, Aunt Em,* or *Uncle Henry.*

1. _____ was an orphan.

2. _____ laughed when she played with her dog.

3. _____ had a long beard and rough boots.

4. _____ had been changed by the sun and the wind.

C VOCABULARY

Complete each sentence with the correct word.

arise	horizon	prairie
attic	in spite of	
cyclone	mass	

1. The line where the sky meets the land is

   called the _____ .

2. A powerful storm with winds that spin

   around is called a _____ .

3. When something _____ , it begins to exist.

4. A room just below the roof of a house is

   called the _____ .

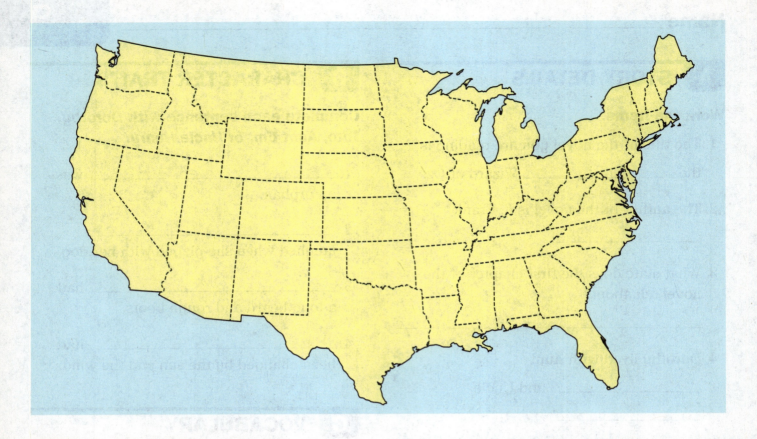

D | MAPS

Work the items.

1. Write **K** on the state where Dorothy lived.

• What is the name of the state where Dorothy lived?

_____

2. Write **M** on the state where Ron took a vacation.

• What is the name of the state where Ron took a vacation?

_____

3. Write **I** on the state where Ron lived.

• What is the name of the state where Ron lived?

_____

E | WORD ENDINGS

Add *ly* to each word. Remember to change the spelling of words that end in *y*.

1. angry _____

2. easy _____

3. tight _____

4. lucky _____

5. peaceful _____

6. entire _____

7. merry _____

GO TO PART E IN YOUR TEXTBOOK

A STORY DETAILS

Work the items.

1. The novel you are reading is called the

   _____ Wizard of Oz.

2. The author of the novel is L. Frank

   _____ .

3. The title of the second chapter is The

   _____ .

4. The main thing that chapter tells about

   is a _____ .

5. Dorothy's house was in the

   _____ of that main thing.

6. When Dorothy was rocked gently, she felt
   like a ▓▓▓▓ .

   a. baby in a cradle

   b. person in a bed

   c. baby on a rocking horse

7. After Toto fell through the trapdoor, one

   of his _____ was sticking
   up through the hole.

8. To prevent accidents, Dorothy ▓▓▓▓
   the trapdoor.

   a. opened   b. closed

   c. got rid of

9. After hours passed, Dorothy
   decided to ▓▓▓▓ .

   a. look out the window

   b. wait calmly

   c. make Toto feel calm

B CHARACTER TRAITS

**Complete each sentence with *Dorothy,
Aunt Em, Uncle Henry,* or *Toto.***

1. _____ closed her eyes and
   fell asleep.

2. _____ went to look after
   the animals.

3. _____ said, "Run for
   the cellar!"

4. _____ felt as if she were
   going up in a balloon.

C WORD ENDINGS

**Add *ly* to each word. Remember to
change the spelling of words that
end in *y.***

1. angry _____

2. careful _____

3. hearty _____

4. pretty _____

D PICTURE CLUES

Work the items.

1. Draw an arrow on the picture above to show which way the cyclone is moving.

• Write **C** on the spinning wind.

• Write **E** on the eye of the cyclone.

2. The spinning wind in the picture can spin up to ▓ miles per hour.

   a. 30   b. 300   c. 3,000

3. The air in the cyclone's eye is ▓ .

   a. still   b. spinning   c. hot

E VOCABULARY

Complete each sentence with the correct word.

| brilliant   deaf   dismally   ripple |

1. The rock band was so loud that the players were becoming _____ .

2. The children had to shield their eyes from the _____ sunlight.

3. The fields began to _____ in the strong wind.

4. The baby cried _____ when it lost its toy.

GO TO PART E IN YOUR TEXTBOOK

Name _____

A STORY DETAILS

Work the items.

1. What color were the Munchkins' clothes?

_____

2. The Munchkins lived in the Land of the 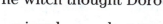.

   a. North   b. South

   c. East   d. West

3. The woman who met Dorothy was a witch.

   a. good   b. bad   c. young

4. She was from the Land of the ____.

   a. North   b. South

   c. East   d. West

5. What color were the witch's clothes?

_____

6. The witch thought Dorothy was a ____.

   a. wizard   b. person from Kansas

   c. sorceress

7. The dead witch was a ____ witch.

   a. good   b. bad   c. young

8. The dead witch had held all the Munchkins in ____ for many years.

   a. chains   b. bondage

   c. cellars

9. The Wizard of Oz lives in the

_____ City.

B CHAPTER TITLES

Write the title of the chapter in which each event occurred. Choose *Kansas*, *The Cyclone*, or *The Munchkins*.

1. Dorothy looked at the prairie.

_____

2. A man in blue greeted Dorothy.

_____

3. Dorothy was high in the air.

_____

4. A sudden jolt awakened Dorothy.

_____

5. Aunt Em ran into the cellar.

_____

C SETTINGS

Complete each sentence with *Kansas* or *The Land of Oz.*

_____ had gray grass.

_____ had gorgeous flowers.

_____ had birds with brilliant feathers.

_____ was a flat prairie.

_____ had large trees.

Copyright © McGraw-Hill Education

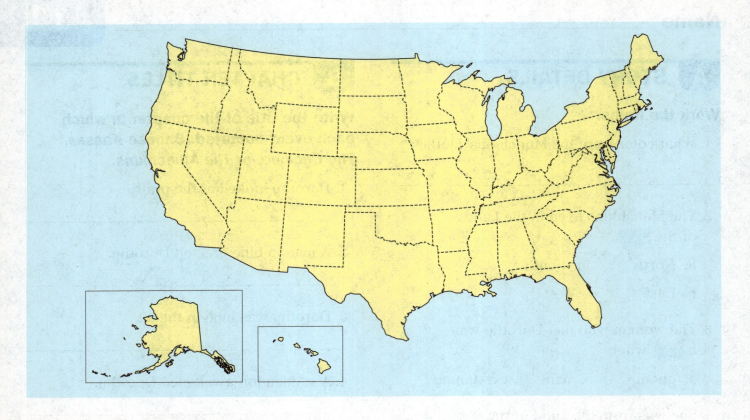

D MAPS

Work the items.

1. Write K on the state where Dorothy lived.

2. What is the name of that state?

   _____

3. A _____ carried Dorothy away from that state.

E VOCABULARY FROM CONTEXT

Complete each sentence with the correct word.

1. We need to _____ about when the bus leaves.

   • forget   • not worry   • inquire

2. The happy music was a

   _____ sound.

   • discouraging   • cheering
   • sad

3. The _____ man had good table manners.

   • wild   • rude   • civilized

F WORD ENDINGS

Write each word with -ly. Remember to change the spelling of words that end in y.

1. awful _____

2. heavy _____

3. natural _____

GO TO PART D IN YOUR TEXTBOOK

A STORY DETAILS

Work the items.

1. What is the title of the fourth chapter?

   _____

2. The main thing this chapter tells about is

   the _____ .

3. Dorothy was anxious to get back to Aunt

   Em and Uncle _____ .

4. To leave the Land of Oz, Dorothy would

   have to cross the Great _____ .

5. Dorothy wore shoes that belonged to the
   Witch of the ▇ .

   a. North   b. South

   c. East   d. West

6. Dorothy was kissed by the Witch
   of the ▇ .

   a. North   b. South

   c. East   d. West

7. That witch kissed Dorothy on her ▇ .

   a. cheek   b. nose

   c. forehead

8. That kiss left a ▇ .

   a. purple bruise

   b. small burn

   c. shiny mark

9. Dorothy took the _____ Road.

B VOCABULARY FROM CONTEXT

Complete each sentence with the correct word.

1. The light was so _____
   they couldn't look at it.

   • dark   • expensive   • brilliant

2. The mother heard the baby's
   _____ and knew he
   was hungry.

   • wail   • rattle   • laughter

3. The cowboys got on their horses and rode

   off across the _____ .

   • ocean   • prairie   • clouds

4. When the little girl knew she was lost,

   she began to cry _____ .

   • happily   • merrily   • dismally

C ATTRIBUTES

• Some of the objects in *The Wonderful
  Wizard of Oz* are magical.

**Complete each sentence with *magical* or
not magical.**

1. The witch's slate is _____ .

2. Dorothy's basket is _____ .

3. Dorothy's gingham dress is

   _____ .

4. Dorothy's silver shoes are

   _____ .

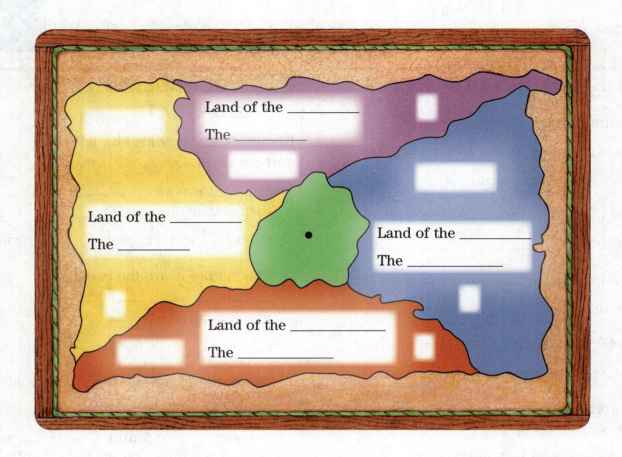

Land of the _____

The _____

Land of the _____

The _____

Land of the _____

The _____

Land of the _____

The _____

D MAPS

Work the items.

1. On the map above, write the name of each land.

2. On each land, write the name of the people who live there.

3. Write **Bad** on the lands that were ruled by bad witches.

4. Write **Good** on the lands that were ruled by good witches.

5. Write **X** on the land that Dorothy is in.

6. Which city does the dot on the map show?

_____

E PERSPECTIVE

Complete each sentence with *knows* or *doesn't know*.

1. Dorothy _____ that Oz is a great wizard.

2. Dorothy _____ that Oz is a man.

3. Dorothy _____ that Oz lives in the Emerald City.

4. Dorothy _____ that Oz will definitely help her.

Copyright © McGraw-Hill Education

GO TO PART E IN YOUR TEXTBOOK

A STORY DETAILS

Work the items.

1. What was the Munchkins' favorite color?

   _____

2. The Munchkins' [ ] had that same color.

   a. hair   b. clothes   c. skin

3. What colors were most things in Kansas?

   _____

4. The people bowed to Dorothy because she had [ ] .

   a. come from Kansas

   b. received a witch's kiss

   c. destroyed an evil witch

5. Boq and his friends had gathered to celebrate [ ] .

   a. the new year

   b. their freedom

   c. the harvest

6. Which two colors did Dorothy's dress have?

   a. blue and white

   b. red and blue

   c. white and red

7. Which color showed that she was a witch?

   _____

8. Which color showed that she was friendly to Munchkins?

   _____

9. Boq thought that Dorothy was a [ ] witch.

   a. fake   b. friendly   c. frightening

B CHARACTER TRAITS

Write or choose the answers.

1. What was the Scarecrow stuffed with that made him so light?

   _____

2. What did the Scarecrow want from Oz?

   _____

3. You couldn't hurt the Scarecrow by stepping on his toes because he [ ] .

   a. wore steel boots.

   b. was empty

   c. was stuffed with straw

4. The only thing the Scarecrow feared was [ ] .

   a. crows   b. fire   c. rain

C SEQUENCING

Number the events in the correct sequence.

_____ The Scarecrow winked at Dorothy.

_____ Dorothy met Boq.

_____ Dorothy and the Scarecrow walked down the road.

_____ A baby played with Toto.

_____ Dorothy lifted the Scarecrow off the pole.

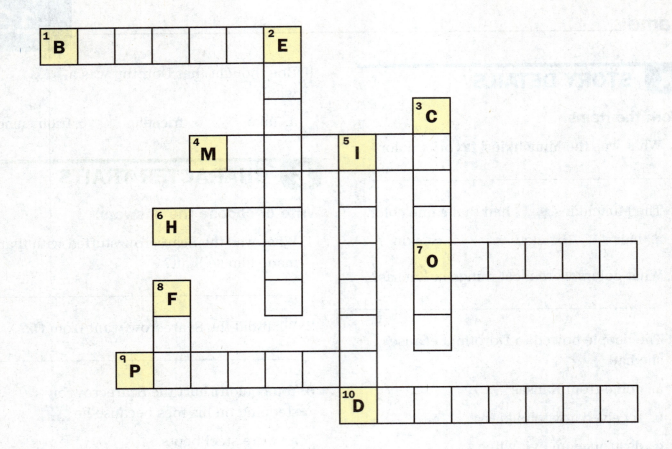

D CROSSWORD PUZZLE

For each item, figure out the vocabulary word that goes in the blank. Then write the word in the puzzle in CAPITAL LETTERS.

ACROSS

1. Dorothy set the Munchkins free from ▮▮▮ .

4. Another word for **happily** is ▮▮▮ .

6. During a storm, you can hear the ▮▮▮ of the wind.

7. A person without any parents is an ▮▮▮ .

9. A grassland with no trees is a ▮▮▮ .

10. Another word for **sadly** is ▮▮▮ .

DOWN

2. ▮▮▮ are expensive green jewels.

3. A strong wind that spins around and around is a ▮▮▮ .

5. Another word for **asked** is ▮▮▮ .

8. Another word for **because** is ▮▮▮ .

GO TO PART D IN YOUR TEXTBOOK

Name ____ **14**

A STORY DETAILS

Work the items.

1. What is the title of Chapter 6?

   ____

2. In this chapter, the ________________ kept falling down.

3. As the travelers walked along, the land became more ______ .

   a. dismal b. beautiful c. blue

4. The Scarecrow was never hungry because he was made of ________________ .

5. If the Scarecrow cut a hole in his mouth, his ________________ would lose its shape.

B PERSPECTIVES

Complete each sentence with *Dorothy, The Scarecrow,* or *Toto.*

1. ________________________ said, "I cannot understand why you want to leave this beautiful country."

2. ________________________ said, "There is no place like home."

3. ________________________ said, "It is fortunate for Kansas that you have brains."

4. ________________________ said, "We people of flesh and blood would rather live there than in any other country."

C SETTINGS

The land has changed since Dorothy began her journey. Complete each sentence with *Before* or *Now*.

1. ________________ there were neat fences by the side of the road.

2. ________________ there are only a few fruit trees.

3. ________________ the country is dismal and lonesome.

4. ________________ there were many round, blue houses.

5. ________________ there are farms that are not well cared for.

D SEQUENCING

Number the events in the correct sequence.

_____ The Witch of the North gave Dorothy some silver shoes.

_____ Dorothy's house landed on top of the Witch of the East.

_____ Dorothy met the Scarecrow.

_____ Dorothy was living in Kansas.

_____ Dorothy met Boq.

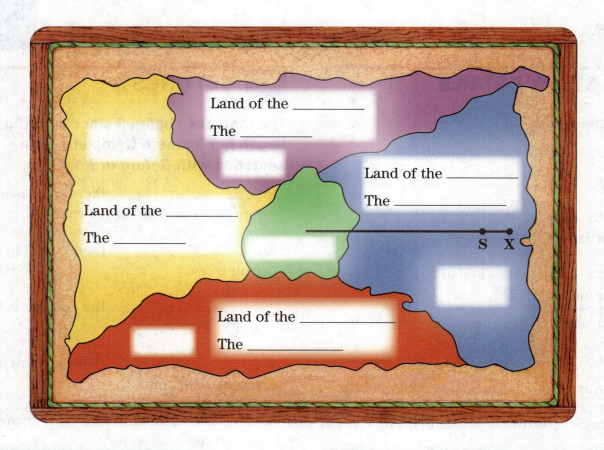

Land of the _____

The _____

Land of the _____

The _____

Land of the _____

The _____

S X

Land of the _____

The _____

E MAPS

Work the items.

1. On the map above, write the name of each land and the name of the people from that land.

2. Write **Bad** on the lands that had bad witches and **Good** on the lands that had good witches.

3. Make a dot on the map to show the city Dorothy wants to visit. Then write the name of the city next to the dot.

4. The **X** shows where Dorothy started out, and the **line** shows the _____ Road.

5. The **S** shows where Dorothy met the _____ in a cornfield.

F VOCABULARY FROM CONTEXT

Complete each sentence with the correct word.

1. They built a huge fire that cast a _____ light.
   - dismal   • brilliant   • cyclone

2. Anthony _____ the books on top of his head.
   - balanced
   - was reading   • looked at

3. Suzanne was happy because her new haircut looked _____ .
   - gorgeous   • awful   • happy

4. The horses pulled and pulled, but the carriage would not _____ .
   - halt   • fly   • budge

GO TO PART D IN YOUR TEXTBOOK

A STORY DETAILS

Work the items.

1. What is the title of Chapter 7?

   _____

2. When the Scarecrow first met Dorothy, how long had he been alive?

   a. one day   b. two days

   c. three days

3. The Scarecrow knows ▆▆ about what happened in the world before he was made.

   a. nothing

   b. some things

   c. everything

4. ▆▆ made the Scarecrow.

   a. Dorothy   b. Boq

   c. A farmer

5. The old crow said the Scarecrow could become a man if he got ▆▆ .

   a. straw   b. brains

   c. muscles

6. What time of day was it when the travelers came to the forest?

   a. evening   b. night

   c. morning

7. The Scarecrow didn't need sleep because he was ▆▆ .

   a. never awake   b. never tired

   c. frozen

8. ▆▆ was making a groaning sound.

   a. Toto   b. The Scarecrow

   c. The Tin Woodman

9. He had been groaning ▆▆ one year.

   a. for exactly   b. for more than

   c. for less than

B VOCABULARY

Complete each sentence with the correct word.

apparent	delicious	serious
balanced	injured	sprinkled
brisk	journey	trot

1. The ceiling was _____ with shining jewels.

2. The dog was not _____ when the car hit it.

3. After an hour, it was _____ he wasn't coming.

4. Mark was in a hurry, so he worked at a _____ pace.

5. The apes thought the bananas were

   _____ .

6. They were packing their suitcases for

   a long _____ .

7. The horse wanted to go faster, so it

   started to _____ .

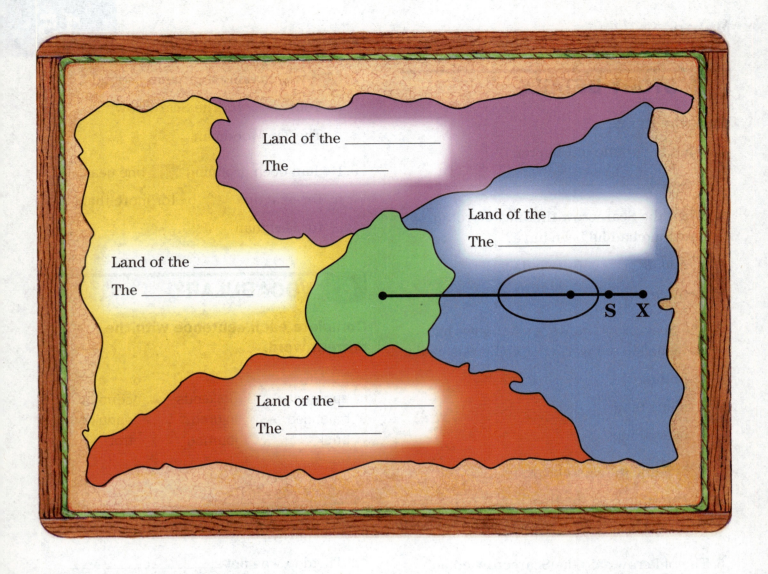

Land of the _____
The _____

Land of the _____
The _____

Land of the _____
The _____

Land of the _____
The _____

S   X

C MAPS

Work the items.

1. On the map above, write the name of each land and the people from that land.

2. The straight line on the map shows where the travelers are going. The circle on the line shows ▨ .

   a. where Dorothy landed

   b. where Dorothy met the Scarecrow

   c. the forest

3. The dot in the middle of the map shows ▨ .

   a. Kansas City

   b. Emerald City

   c. Dorothy's house

4. Which direction are the travelers going?

   _____

5. The **S** shows where Dorothy met the ▨ .

   a. Scarecrow   b. sorceress

   c. Witch of the North

GO TO PART D IN YOUR TEXTBOOK

A STORY DETAILS

Work the items.

1. What is the title of Chapter 8?

   _____

2. The Tin Woodman couldn't move when Dorothy found him because he was ▭ .

   a. rusted   b. in shock

   c. frozen

3. What liquid did Dorothy get for the Tin Woodman?

   _____

4. What liquid could make the Tin Woodman rust again?

   _____

5. The Tin Woodman wanted to marry ▭ .

   a. Dorothy

   b. the Tin Woodwoman

   c. a Munchkin girl

6. The Witch of the ▭ put a spell on the Tin Woodman's axe.

   a. South   b. West

   c. East

7. What cut off parts of the Tin Woodman's body?

   a. an axe   b. a saw

   c. a sword

8. The Tin Woodman was missing ▭ .

   a. brains   b. courage

   c. a heart

B VOCABULARY

Complete each sentence with the correct word.

balanced	injured	solemn
crops	represented	sorceress
entertained	resolved	suspected
gorgeous		

1. They laughed because they were

   _____ .

2. The sunset was pretty because it

   had _____ colors.

3. Farmers harvest their

   _____ in the fall.

4. Selena held a tray in each hand and

   carefully _____ them.

5. Yuja _____ that she would do a better job the next time.

6. The artist drew lines that

   _____ a horse.

7. The people at the funeral looked very

   _____ .

8. The police officer _____ that the man was lying.

C | CHARACTER STATEMENTS

**Complete each sentence with *Dorothy,
The Scarecrow,* or *The Tin Woodman.***

1. _____ said,
"I might have stood there always if you
had not come along."

2. _____ said,
"I want Oz to send me back to Kansas."

3. _____ said,
"My head is stuffed with straw."

4. _____ said,
"There was a Munchkin girl who was so
beautiful that I soon grew to love her."

5. _____ said,
"Happiness is the best thing in the world."

6. _____ said,
"A fool would not know what to do with
a heart if he had one."

D | SETTINGS

**Complete each sentence with *Kansas,
The Munchkins,* or *The forest.***

1. _____ had
gray grass.

2. _____ had
branches growing over the road.

3. _____ had
blue fences beside the road.

4. _____ had
roads that were well cared for.

5. _____ had
round houses.

6. _____ had
cracked land.

7. _____ had
thick trees everywhere.

E | EVIDENCE

**Dorothy knows only a few things about
the Wizard of Oz. Complete each sentence
with *knows* or *doesn't know.***

1. Dorothy

_____ that Oz
is more powerful than the witches.

2. Dorothy

_____ that Oz
lives in the Emerald City.

3. Dorothy

_____ if Oz
will send her back to Kansas.

4. Dorothy

_____ if Oz
will give the Scarecrow brains.

5. Dorothy

_____ that Oz
is a wizard.

GO TO PART D IN YOUR TEXTBOOK

Name _____

A STORY DETAILS

Work the items.

1. What is the title of Chapter 9?

   _____

2. Who slapped the Lion on the nose?

   _____

3. A lion is supposed to act ▨.
   a. cowardly   b. bravely
   c. politely

4. The Lion is supposed to be the King of _____ .

5. The Lion made other animals run away by ▨.
   a. roaring   b. biting them
   c. crying

6. If the other animals had tried to fight, the Lion would have ▨.
   a. eaten them   b. roared louder
   c. run away

7. After the Tin Woodman stepped on the beetle, he began to ▨.
   a. rub his foot   b. cry
   c. hop

8. What happened to the Tin Woodman's jaws after he stepped on the beetle?
   a. They rusted together.
   b. They opened wide.
   c. He used them to eat the beetle.

9. How did the Scarecrow fix the Tin Woodman's jaws?
   a. He pried them open.
   b. He wrapped them with a bandage.
   c. He oiled them.

B VOCABULARY

Complete each sentence with the correct word.

| apparent | merrily | sprinkled |
| delicious | represented | suspected |

1. Jean ate spoonful after spoonful of the _____ ice cream.

2. Karim saw the clouds and _____ it was going to rain.

3. Paintings by cave people _____ the animals they hunted.

4. The baker _____ nuts over the cake.

Copyright © McGraw-Hill Education

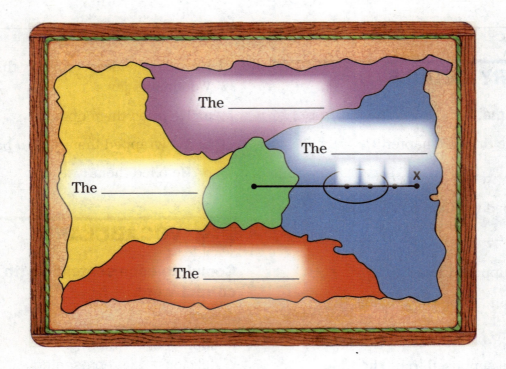

The _____

The _____

The _____

The _____

X

C MAPS

Work the Items.

1. On the map above, write the name of the people who live in each land.

2. The **X** shows where Dorothy started, and the **line** shows the road she is on. What is that road made out of?

   _____

3. Write **S** on the dot that shows where Dorothy met the Scarecrow.

4. Write **T** on the dot that shows where Dorothy met the Tin Woodman.

5. Write **L** on the dot that shows where Dorothy met the Lion.

6. What kind of place does the circle show?

   a. a forest   b. a field   c. a mountain

7. In which direction are the travelers walking?

   _____

D CHARACTER STATEMENTS

**Complete each sentence with *Dorothy,
The Scarecrow, The Tin Woodman,* or
*The Lion.***

1. _____ said,
   "I am not afraid so long as I have my oilcan."

2. _____ said,
   "Don't you dare bite Toto."

3. _____ said,
   "I know that I am a coward."

4. _____ said,
   "All the other animals expect me to be brave."

GO TO PART D IN YOUR TEXTBOOK

A STORY DETAILS

Work the items.

1. The Cowardly Lion offered to kill a deer for Dorothy so she could ▮▮▮ .

   a. get the antlers   b. have food to eat

   c. make a coat

2. The _____ begged the Cowardly Lion not to kill the deer.

3. Why did the Scarecrow stay away from the fire?

   a. He was already warm.

   b. He didn't want to burn up.

   c. It was too bright for him.

4. The _____ figured out how to get across the first ditch.

5. The _____ carried the travelers across the first ditch.

6. The _____ chopped down the tree at the second ditch.

7. When the Kalidahs appeared, the Cowardly Lion ▮▮▮ .

   a. roared   b. ran away

   c. started crying

8. The Kalidahs stopped for an instant because they ▮▮▮ .

   a. needed to catch their breath

   b. had to come up with a plan

   c. were surprised

B MAPS

Pretend you are in the Emerald City. Write which direction you would go to reach each group of people.

1. Quadlings _____

2. Winkies _____

3. Munchkins _____

4. Gillikins _____

C SETTINGS

Complete each sentence with *Kansas, the Land of the Munchkins,* or *the forest.*

1. In _____, the wind howled across the prairie.

2. In _____, there were deep ditches with ragged rocks on the bottom.

3. In _____, the sun baked the land into a gray mass.

4. In _____, there were neat blue fences beside the road.

5. In _____, the road was covered with branches.

D CHAPTER TITLES

Write the title of the chapter for each event. Choose _Kansas_, _The Tin Woodman_, or _The Kalidahs._

1. The Lion roared at two great beasts.

_____

2. The Tin Woodman told his story.

_____

3. Uncle Henry looked anxiously at the sky.

_____

4. Dorothy found a can with oil in it.

_____

E SEQUENCING

Number the events in the correct sequence.

_____ The Lion jumped across a ditch.

_____ The Kalidahs fell to the bottom of the ditch.

_____ The travelers camped out under a large tree.

_____ The Lion pushed a tree across a ditch.

_____ The Kalidahs chased the travelers across a tree.

F VOCABULARY

Complete each sentence with the correct word.

amused	mystery	solemn
civilized	represented	suspected
companion	satisfaction	

1. The clown _____ them and made them laugh.

2. The five-pointed object

_____ a star.

3. After completing the climb, Dora felt great

_____ .

4. The cat was her only _____ .

5. The strange noises in the house at night

were a _____ to them.

GO TO PART D IN YOUR TEXTBOOK

Name _____

A FACT GAME

Scorecard

1	2	3	4	5	6	7	8	9	10
11	12	13	14	15	16	17	18	19	20
21	22	23	24	25	26	27	28	29	30

2. Tell which direction each arrow points. Start with arrow A.

A   B   C   D   E

→   ↓   ←   ↑   ↓

3. Answer these questions about the map below.

   a. Which country does the map show?

   b. Which state has an A on it?

4. Tell which group of people lived in each land.

   a. The Land of the North

   b. The Land of the South

   c. The Land of the West

   d. The Land of the East

5. Tell whether Dorothy saw each thing in *Kansas* or in the *Land of Oz*.

   a. Gray grass

   b. Round blue houses

   c. Beautiful flowers

   d. Flat prairie

6. Answer these questions about the Land of Oz.

   a. What surrounded the Land of Oz?

   b. What city was in the middle of the Land of Oz?

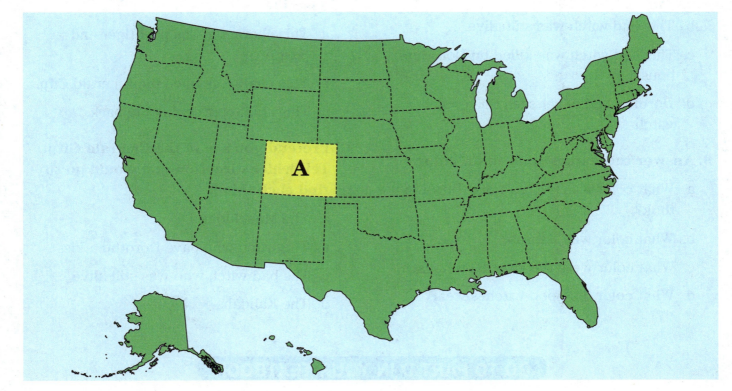

7. Answer these questions about the picture above.

a. What does the picture show?

b. What is the name of part A?

8. Tell which land each witch is from.

a. This good witch gave Dorothy a kiss.

b. This bad witch was still alive.

c. This bad witch was killed by Dorothy's house.

d. Dorothy had never seen this good witch.

9. Answer these questions about color.

a. What color was the road that Dorothy took?

b. What color was Kansas?

c. What color were the Munchkin houses?

d. What color did good witches wear?

10. Tell which character wanted each thing.

a. Brains

b. Courage

c. A trip back to Kansas

d. A heart

11. Tell which character each statement describes.

a. This character was part tiger and part bear.

b. This character ruled the Emerald City.

c. This character could only bark.

12. Pretend you are in the Emerald City. Tell which direction you would go to find each thing.

a. The Munchkins

b. The witch who gave Dorothy a kiss

c. The bad witch who was still alive

d. The Kalidahs

GO TO PART D IN YOUR TEXTBOOK

A STORY DETAILS

Work the items.

1. The _____ pulled the raft toward the shore by swimming.

2. After the travelers reached the shore, they decided to walk back to the ▆ .
   a. Emerald City   b. Yellow Brick Road
   c. Munchkins

3. The bird that carried the Scarecrow back to shore was a _____ .

4. What color were the flowers with the powerful odor?
   a. scarlet   b. starlet
   c. scarred

5. Animals who breathe the odor of those flowers ▆ .
   a. smell nice   b. sneeze
   c. fall asleep

6. Animals who are not carried away from the flowers can ▆ .
   a. start coughing   b. sleep forever
   c. smell bad

7. At the end of the chapter, Dorothy was lying beside the ▆ .
   a. field of flowers   b. river
   c. Yellow Brick Road

8. What was the air like in that spot?
   a. stale   b. poisonous
   c. fresh

B SETTINGS

Complete each sentence with *forest, river,* or *field of flowers*.

1. In the _____,
   you smell something and fall asleep.

2. In the _____,
   you float downstream.

3. In the _____,
   you get chased by Kalidahs.

4. In the _____,
   you sleep forever.

5. In the _____,
   you steer a raft.

C VOCABULARY MATCHING

Connect each word in the left column with the correct meaning in the right column.

1. motionless   comforted
2. remarkable   unusual
3. passage   sadness
4. sorrow   satisfaction
5. surprise   path
6. misfortune   dull
7. dreary   astonish
                     not moving
                     bad luck

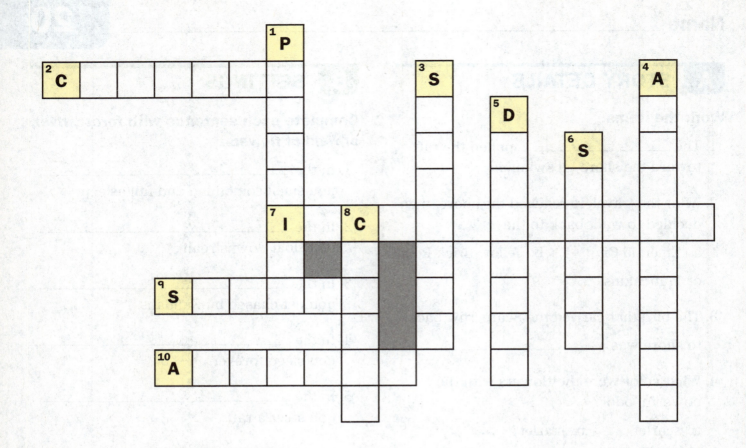

D CROSSWORD PUZZLE

For each item, figure out which vocabulary word goes in the blank. Then write the word in the puzzle in CAPITAL LETTERS.

Across

2. A friend is a ▓▓▓ .

7. Another word for **annoying** is ▓▓▓ .

9. Another word for **sadness** is ▓▓▓ .

10. When you are clumsy, you are ▓▓▓ .

Down

1. Another word for **strange** is ▓▓▓ .

3. Another word for **marvelous** is ▓▓▓ .

4. When you are really surprised, you are ▓▓▓ .

5. When you are left alone, you feel ▓▓▓ .

6. When it is cold, your body begins to ▓▓▓ .

8. When you are not brave, you are a ▓▓▓ .

E SEQUENCING

Number the events in the correct sequence.

_____ The travelers came to a field of flowers.

_____ The Stork saved the Scarecrow.

_____ The Lion pulled the raft to shore.

_____ The Lion fell asleep.

_____ Dorothy and Toto fell asleep.

GO TO PART C IN YOUR TEXTBOOK

A STORY DETAILS

Work the items.

1. At the beginning of the chapter, a

   _____ was

   chasing the Queen.

2. Which character saved the Queen?

   a. Dorothy   b. Scarecrow

   c. Tin Woodman

3. How many mice did the Queen command?

   a. dozens   b. hundreds

   c. thousands

4. Which character thought of something the mice could do for the travelers?

   a. Dorothy   b. the Scarecrow

   c. the Tin Woodman

5. The mice were afraid of saving the Lion because they thought he would ▨ .

   a. crush them   b. eat them

   c. put them in prison

6. There was no reason to be afraid of the Lion because he was really a ▨ .

   a. cat   b. coward

   c. king

7. The _____

   made a cart for the Lion.

8. At the end of the chapter, the Queen gave

   Dorothy a _____ .

B SEQUENCING

Number the events in the correct sequence.

_____ The mice pulled the cart.

_____ The Tin Woodman chopped down some trees.

_____ The Queen promised to help the travelers again.

_____ The Scarecrow came up with a plan to save the Lion.

_____ The Tin Woodman saved the Queen.

C VOCABULARY

Complete each sentence with the correct word.

coward	inconvenient	shivered
fortunate	marvelous	strides

1. The kitten _____ because of the cold.

2. The mice were _____ that Toto could not chase them.

3. The Lion had no courage, so he was a

   _____ .

4. People ran away from the Kalidahs with

   long _____ .

5. The rainbow was so _____ that everyone stared at it.

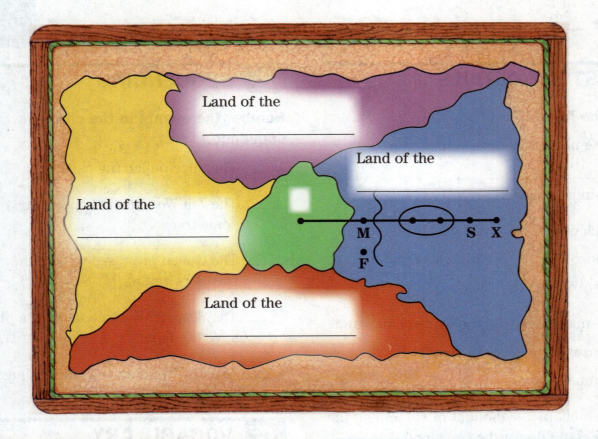

Land of the _____

Land of the _____

Land of the _____

Land of the _____

M   S   X

F

D MAPS

Work the items.

1. Complete the name of each land on the map.

2. Write **E** on the dot that shows the Emerald City.

3. The circle around the two dots shows the _____ .

4. The wavy line next to the circle shows the _____ .

5. The **F** shows the place where the Lion fell asleep. What grew in that place?

   _____

6. Which animals did the travelers meet at **M**?

   _____

E CHARACTER TRAITS

Complete each sentence with *Dorothy, The Tin Woodman, The Lion,* or *The Scarecrow*.

1. _____ came from Kansas.

2. _____ stunned a wildcat.

3. _____ was put on a cart.

4. _____ built a raft and a cart.

5. _____ ate raw meat.

GO TO PART C IN YOUR TEXTBOOK

Name ______________________________

A STORY DETAILS

Work the items.

1. What color are houses in the Land of the Munchkins?

   ____

2. What color are houses near the Emerald City?

   ____

3. The man with the injured leg had never seen Oz because Oz never lets anyone come into his ____ .

   a. presence   b. presents

   c. present

4. The man thought that Oz could help the Scarecrow because Oz has more

   ______________ than he needs.

5. The man thought that Oz could help the Tin Woodman because Oz has a large collection of ______________ .

6. The man thought that Oz could help the Lion because Oz has a great pot of

   ______________ .

7. What color was the glow that the travelers saw in the sky?

   ____

8. The ______________ City caused the glow.

9. That city was surrounded by a great

   ______________ .

B VOCABULARY MATCHING

Connect each word in the left column with the correct meaning in the right column.

1. clumsiness	peculiar
2. horrible	comrade
3. deserted	dreadful
4. strange	gloomy
5. tight-fitting	snug
6. crouched	bent down
7. dismal	declared
	awkwardness
	abandoned

C SEQUENCING

Number the events in the correct sequence.

____ The Stork rescued the Scarecrow.

____ The travelers talked to a man with an injured leg.

____ The Lion jumped across a wide ditch.

____ The travelers entered the Emerald City.

____ The Tin Woodman saved the Queen of the Mice.

D POINT OF VIEW

Complete each sentence with *heard* or *didn't hear*.

1. Dorothy _____ someone say, "Oz is more powerful than all the witches."

2. Dorothy _____ someone say, "Oz always looks like a monster."

3. Dorothy _____ someone say, "Oz never lets anyone see him."

4. Dorothy _____ someone say, "Oz is afraid of the witches."

5. Dorothy _____ someone say, "Many people have seen Oz."

6. Dorothy _____ someone say, "No one knows what Oz's real form is."

7. Dorothy _____ someone say, "Oz can take any form he wants."

8. Dorothy _____ someone say, "Oz walks around the Emerald City."

9. Dorothy _____ someone say, "Oz has a collection of hearts."

E SETTINGS

Complete each sentence with *of the East*, *near Emerald City*, or *called Kansas*.

1. In the Land

_____ , the grass was gray, and the wind howled.

2. In the Land

_____ , people wore green hats.

3. In the Land

_____ , there were round houses with blue domes.

4. In the Land

_____ , there were blue fences by the side of the road.

5. In the Land

_____ , green fences lined the road.

6. In the Land

_____ , the sky glowed in the same color as the houses.

GO TO PART C IN YOUR TEXTBOOK

Name ______________________________ 23

A STORY DETAILS

Work the items.

1. In the Emerald City, ____ of the people wore spectacles.
   a. none b. only a few
   c. all

2. What color was the glass in the spectacles?
   ____

3. The Guardian said the spectacles would protect the travelers from the ____ of the Emerald City.
   a. gloom b. brightness
   c. heat

4. What kind of stone were the houses and sidewalks made of?
   ____

5. What kind of gem was studded everywhere?
   ____

6. The Palace of Oz was ____ of the city.
   a. on the edge b. outside
   c. in the middle

7. Oz said he would admit only ____ each day.
   a. one traveler b. three travelers
   c. five travelers

8. Which travelers slept that night?
   a. Dorothy b. Toto
   c. Scarecrow d. Tin Woodman
   e. Cowardly Lion

9. Which travelers did not sleep?
   a. Dorothy b. Toto
   c. Scarecrow d. Tin Woodman
   e. Cowardly Lion

B VOCABULARY

Complete each sentence with the correct word.

apparent	dazzled	peculiar
companion	fortunate	refreshed

1. After a good night's rest, Todd felt strong and ______________ .
2. Kata's jewels were so brilliant that they ______________ people.
3. When Kumar won the lottery, he realized how ______________ he was.
4. A dog can be a perfect ______________ for a walk in the woods.
5. Everyone was puzzled by the ______________ odor.

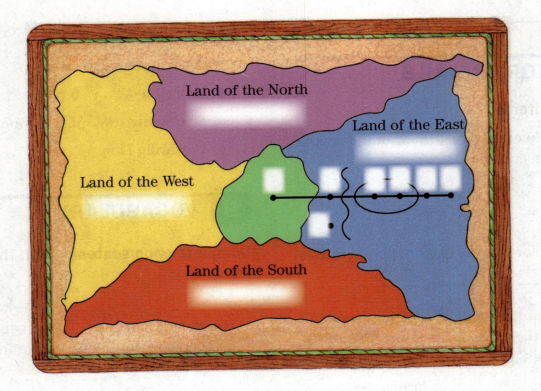

Land of the North

Land of the East

Land of the West

Land of the South

C MAPS

1. Write **Bad** on the lands that had bad witches. Write **Good** on the lands that had good witches.

2. Write **S** on the dot where Dorothy met a man who needed brains.

3. Write **E** on the dot where a wizard lived.

4. Write **M** on the dot where travelers met thousands of small animals.

5. Write **T** on the dot where Dorothy met a man who needed a heart.

6. Write **L** on the dot where Dorothy met an animal that needed courage.

7. Write **X** on the dot where Dorothy's house landed.

8. Write **F** on the dot where Dorothy smelled a strong odor.

D SETTINGS

Complete each sentence with *Emerald City, field of flowers,* or *river*.

1. In the _____ , you see a room with a high arched ceiling.

2. In the _____ , you see field mice pulling a cart.

3. In the _____ , you are carried by a swift current.

4. In the _____ , you see people wearing green spectacles.

5. In the _____ , you see travelers on a raft.

6. In the _____ , you see sidewalks made of marble.

GO TO PART C IN YOUR TEXTBOOK

Name ______________________________ 24

A STORY DETAILS

Work the items.

1. What shape was the throne room?
   a. round b. square
   c. rectangular

2. The walls, ceilings, and floor of the throne room were covered by
   ________________ .

3. The throne was made out of green ______ .
   a. sandstone b. marble
   c. granite

4. Floating above the throne was an enormous ________________ .

5. Oz was interested in the silver ________________ that Dorothy was wearing.

6. Oz was also interested in the mark left by the witch's ________________ on Dorothy's face.

7. Dorothy wanted Oz to send her back to ________________ .

8. Oz wanted Dorothy to ______ the Wicked Witch of the West.
   a. capture b. charm
   c. kill

B SEQUENCING

Number the events in the correct sequence.

_____ Dorothy entered the throne room.

_____ Dorothy put on a green dress.

_____ Dorothy told Oz that she wanted to go back to Kansas.

_____ Oz told Dorothy to kill the Wicked Witch of the West.

_____ Oz asked Dorothy how she got the silver shoes.

C CHARACTER STATEMENTS

Complete each sentence with *Dorothy, Oz,* or *The green girl.*

1. ______________________________ said, "Help me and I will help you."

2. ______________________________ said, "I never killed anything willingly."

3. ______________________________ said, "I am great and terrible."

4. ______________________________ said, "In this country, people must pay for everything they get."

5. ______________________________ said, "I am small and meek."

D CHARACTER TRAITS

Complete each sentence with *North, East, South,* or *West.*

1. Oz ordered Dorothy to kill the Witch of the

   _____ .

2. The Witch of the _____
   lived with the Gillikins.

3. The silver shoes belonged to the Witch of

   the _____ .

4. The Witch of the _____
   lived with the Winkies.

5. The Witch of the _____
   gave Dorothy a kiss on the forehead.

6. The Witch of the _____
   lived with the Quadlings.

E VOCABULARY MATCHING

Connect each word in the left column with the correct meaning in the right column.

1. horrible   crouch

2. delightful   dismal

3. hardly   wonderful

4. group   scarlet

5. gloomy   scarcely

6. scent   smell

7. shy   so

8. therefore   timid

                     cluster

                     dreadful

GO TO PART C IN YOUR TEXTBOOK

A STORY DETAILS

Work the items.

1. What form did Oz take for the Scarecrow?

   a. ball of fire   b. lovely lady

   c. terrible beast   d. floating head

2. Oz agreed to give the Scarecrow

   _____ .

3. But first the Scarecrow has to kill the

   Wicked Witch of the _____ .

4. What form did Oz take for the Tin Woodman?

   a. ball of fire   b. lovely lady

   c. terrible beast   d. floating head

5. If the Tin Woodman doesn't kill the witch,

   he will never have a _____ .

6. What form did Oz take for the Lion?

   a. ball of fire   b. lovely lady

   c. terrible beast   d. floating head

7. If the Lion doesn't kill the witch, he will

   never have _____ .

8. Which direction must the travelers go to reach the Wicked Witch?

   _____

B CHARACTER TRAITS

Complete each sentence with *Lion*, *Scarecrow*, or *Woodman*.

1. The _____ didn't have the courage to kill the Wicked Witch.

2. The _____ didn't have enough brains to kill the Wicked Witch.

3. The _____ didn't have the heart to kill the Wicked Witch.

4. The _____ saw Oz as a ball of fire.

5. The _____ wanted to see Oz as a lovely lady.

C POINT OF VIEW

Complete each sentence with *knows* or *doesn't know*.

1. Dorothy _____ that Oz lives in the Emerald City.

2. Dorothy _____ that Oz can take any form he wants.

3. Dorothy _____ that the real Oz is a floating head.

4. Dorothy _____ that Oz appears in the throne room.

5. Dorothy _____ that Oz will send her back to Kansas.

D SEQUENCING

Number the events in the correct sequence.

_____ Oz took the form of a ball of fire.

_____ The Guardian of the Gates locked green spectacles on the travelers.

_____ The travelers decided to kill the Wicked Witch of the West.

_____ Oz took the form of a giant head.

E SETTINGS

Complete each sentence with *forest,* *field of flowers,* or *Emerald City.*

1. In the _____, you sleep forever.

2. In the _____, you walk by a palace.

3. In the _____, you jump over a wide ditch.

4. In the _____, you walk on marble sidewalks.

5. In the _____, you smell something that makes you sleepy.

6. In the _____, you pay with green money.

7. In the _____, you get chased by Kalidahs.

8. In the _____, you have to wear glasses all day long.

GO TO PART C IN YOUR TEXTBOOK

A STORY DETAILS

Work the items.

1. When Dorothy left the Emerald City, her green dress turned _____ .

2. The Witch could see far because her eye was like a _____ .

3. The Witch used ▨ to command the Winged Monkeys.

    a. a golden cap   b. the silver shoes

    c. a broom

4. The Winged Monkeys dropped the Tin Woodman over a plain covered with ▨ .

    a. sharp rocks   b. tall trees

    c. green grass

5. The bundle that the Winged Monkeys threw into a tree contained the Scarecrow's ▨ .

    a. straw   b. brains   c. clothes

6. Why didn't the Winged Monkeys kill the Lion?

    a. They were afraid of him.

    b. They had to bring him back alive.

    c. The Lion escaped.

7. The mark on Dorothy's forehead showed that she was protected by the Power of

    _____ .

8. Which person knew how to use the power of the silver shoes?

    a. Dorothy   b. Oz

    c. The Witch of the West

9. The shoes had belonged to the Witch of the ▨ .

    a. North   b. South

    c. East   d. West

B VOCABULARY

Complete each sentence with the correct word.

admitted	journey	permit
amused	meek	preferred
enormous	odor	

1. Latasha held the flowers and breathed in their magnificent _____ .

2. The guard would not _____ anybody to go inside the city.

3. After Rhoda was _____ to the office, she sat and waited.

4. The hole was so _____ that they couldn't see the bottom.

5. He was a _____ little boy who never said much.

6. Diana liked to work, but she _____ to sleep.

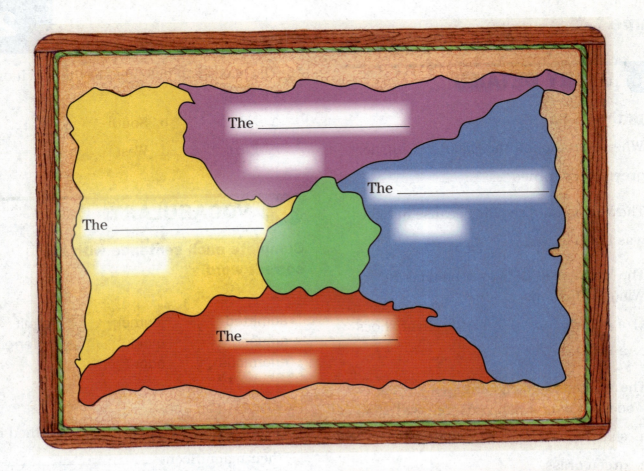

The _____

The _____

The _____

The _____

C MAPS

Work the items.

1. On the map above, write which people lived in each land.

2. Write **good** on the lands that had good witches.

3. Write **house** on the land where a house killed a bad witch.

4. Write **bad** on the land that still had a bad witch.

5. Make a dot to show the Emerald City.

6. Draw an arrow from the dot to show which way the travelers went after they left the Emerald City.

D CHARACTER STATEMENTS

Complete each sentence with *Dorothy, The Lion, The Witch,* or *The Woodman.*

1. _____ said, "I don't have the heart to harm even a Witch."

2. _____ said, "I am too afraid to kill the Witch."

3. _____ said, "Oz will not send me home until the Witch is dead."

4. _____ said, "Fly away and seize the travelers!"

5. _____ said, "I will make an end of you."

GO TO PART C IN YOUR TEXTBOOK

A STORY DETAILS

Work the items.

1. The Witch wanted the silver shoes because she ▉▉▉ .

   a. had lost them years ago

   b. had used up the power of the golden cap

   c. wanted to conquer Oz

2. The Witch didn't take the shoes when Dorothy was asleep because ▉▉▉ .

   a. the Witch couldn't see in the dark

   b. Dorothy hid them

   c. the Witch was afraid of the dark

3. The Witch didn't take the shoes when Dorothy was bathing because ▉▉▉ .

   a. Dorothy put the shoes in the bathtub

   b. the Witch was afraid of water

   c. Dorothy never bathed

4. The Witch put an iron ▉▉▉ in the middle of the kitchen floor.

   a. bar   b. pot   c. shoe

5. Dorothy lost one of the silver shoes when she ▉▉▉ .

   a. tried to run away

   b. tripped and fell down

   c. got stuck in the mud

6. The Witch melted when Dorothy threw _____ on her.

7. Dorothy set the Lion, the Winkies and the _____ free from bondage.

8. The Winkie _____ fixed the Tin Woodman's body.

B VOCABULARY

Complete each sentence with the correct word.

advanced	requested	slightest
meek	scent	weep
presence		

1. The rotten eggs had a bad _____ .

2. The king was bored and welcomed the clown's _____ .

3. When you are very sad, you sometimes _____ loudly.

4. The girl with sharp ears could hear the _____ sound.

5. The snail _____ slowly across the lawn.

6. Jan _____ a salad and a glass of milk.

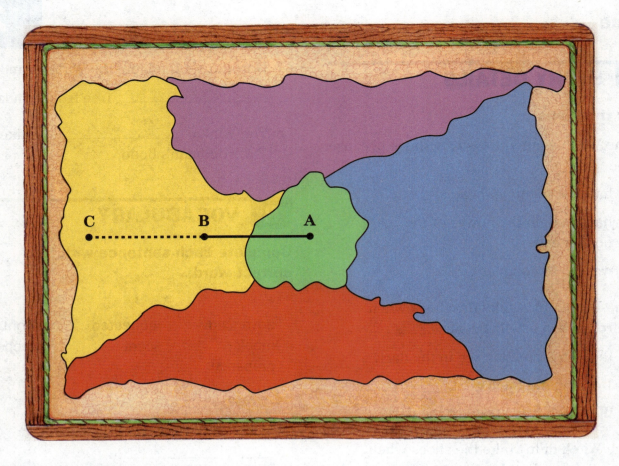

C | MAPS

Work the items.

1. Dot **A** shows the

   _____ .

2. Dot **B** shows where the travelers were attacked by the Winged

   _____ .

3. Dot **C** shows where the Wicked Witch of

   the _____ lived.

4. The solid line shows that Dorothy traveled from place **A** to place **B** by ▨ .

   a. land   b. water   c. air

5. The dotted line shows that Dorothy traveled from place **B** to place **C** by ▨ .

   a. land   b. water   c. air

D | SEQUENCING

Number the events in the correct sequence.

_____ Dorothy freed the Lion.

_____ The Witch made an iron bar invisible.

_____ Dorothy threw a bucket of water at the Witch.

_____ Tinsmiths fixed the Tin Woodman.

_____ The Witch melted away.

GO TO PART C IN YOUR TEXTBOOK

A STORY DETAILS

Work the item.

1. Which direction was the Emerald City from the witch's castle?

   _____

2. To get to the Emerald City, the travelers would have to go toward the ▩.

   a. stars   b. setting sun

   c. rising sun

3. The travelers got lost at ▩, when the sun was not in the east or west.

   a. midnight   b. dusk   c. noon

4. Dorothy used her whistle to call the ▩.

   a. field mice   b. Winged Monkeys

   c. Winkies

5. The travelers had met those characters in the ▩.

   a. forest   b. field of flowers

   c. Emerald City

6. Dorothy asked the Winged Monkeys to take the travelers to the

   _____ .

7. The Winged Monkeys had to obey Dorothy because she was wearing the ▩.

   a. silver shoes   b. golden cap

   c. whistle

8. When Oz would not see the travelers, the Scarecrow threatened to call the

   _____ .

9. Oz was frightened by the Scarecrow's threat because ▩.

   a. those animals had defeated him before

   b. the Winkies had a powerful army

   c. he was scared of mice

B CHARACTER STATEMENTS

Complete each sentence with *Dorothy, The King of the Monkeys, The Lion, The Queen of the Mice, The Scarecrow,* or *The Tin Woodman.*

1. _____ said, "I am happy that my dents were fixed."

2. _____ said, "There is no place like home."

3. _____ said, "I really like my new straw."

4. _____ said, "I think I'll try on this golden cap."

5. _____ said, "We must obey your commands three times."

6. _____ said, "Just blow on the whistle whenever you need our help."

C VOCABULARY

Complete each sentence with the correct word.

cunning	requested	studded
desperately	seized	tempt
meek	singed	terror

1. Victor deserved more money, but he was too _____ to ask for it.

2. Rosa _____ soup and a sandwich.

3. The paper was black after being _____ in the fire.

4. The police _____ the crook and wouldn't let him go.

5. Max held the meat near the fence and tried to _____ the dog.

6. The anxious traveler _____ wanted to catch the train.

7. The _____ thief could steal anything.

D CHARACTER TRAITS

Complete each sentence with *Kalidahs, Munchkins, Winged Monkeys,* or *Winkies.*

1. The _____ had to obey the owner of the cap.

2. The _____ wore blue hats.

3. The _____ wore yellow clothes.

4. The _____ liked to make mischief.

5. The _____ had heads like tigers and bodies like bears.

6. The _____ had farms in the Land of the East.

GO TO PART C IN YOUR TEXTBOOK

Name _____

A   FACT GAME

Scorecard

1	2	3	4	5	6	7	8	9	10
11	12	13	14	15	16	17	18	19	20
21	22	23	24	25	26	27	28	29	30

2. Tell which direction each arrow points. Start with arrow A.

A   B   C   D   E

↓   ←   ←   ↓   →

3. Answer these questions about the picture below.

   a. What object does the picture show?

   b. What is the name of part Z?

4. Tell which land each group of people lived in.

   a. Gillikins

   b. Quadlings

   c. Winkies

   d. Munchkins

5. Tell which color each thing is.

   a. Munchkin hats

   b. Emerald City

   c. Kansas

   d. Winkie hats

6. Tell which character could have made each statement.

   a. "There is no place like home."

   b. "A match might burn my straw."

   c. "I will rust if I cry."

   d. "I am supposed to be the King of Beasts."

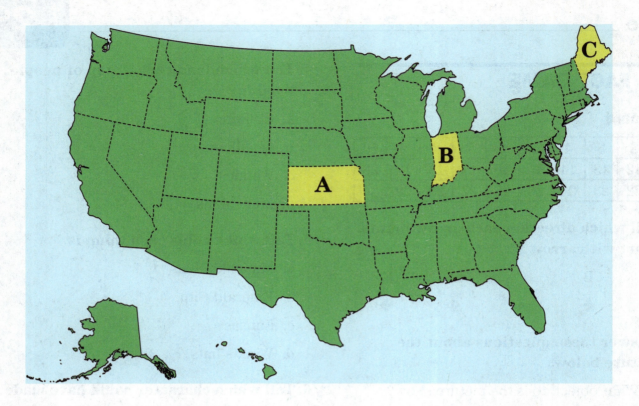

7. Answer these questions about the map.

   a. What is the name of state **A**?

   b. What is the name of state **B**?

   c. What is the name of state **C**?

8. Pretend you are in the Emerald City. Tell which direction you would go to find each thing.

   a. A forest with Kalidahs in it

   b. A castle that was once ruled by an evil witch

   c. A house that landed from the sky

   d. The witch who ruled over the Quadlings

9. Answer these questions.

   a. Which city is in the middle of the Land of Oz?

   b. Who rules that city?

   c. What surrounds the Land of Oz?

10. Answer these questions.

   a. Which people slaved for the Wicked Witch of the West?

   b. Which animals pulled a cart to save the Lion?

   c. Which animals chased the travelers across a ditch?

11. Tell which event happened *first,* then *second,* then *third.*

   a. Dorothy killed the Witch of the West.

   b. Dorothy fell asleep in a field of flowers.

   c. Dorothy met the Scarecrow.

12. Tell which land each witch is from.

   a. This witch had only one eye.

   b. This witch was killed by a house.

   c. This witch lived with the Gillikins.

GO TO PART C IN YOUR TEXTBOOK

A STORY DETAILS

Work the items.

1. Oz was able to make his voice come out of the giant head because he was a

    _____ .

2. What did Oz use to make the beast that the Tin Woodman saw?

    a. colored paper

    b. carpet samples

    c. animal skins

3. The ball of fire was actually a ball of

    _____ .

4. When Oz worked for a circus, he flew in a

    _____ .

5. Was the Emerald City really green?

    _____

6. The people thought the Emerald City was green because ▪▪▪ .

    a. they wore green spectacles

    b. they had green eyes

    c. it was really green

7. If the bad witches had known the truth about Oz's power, they would have tried to ▪▪▪ .

    a. protect themselves

    b. destroy him

    c. run away

8. Oz told the Lion that what he really needed was ▪▪▪ .

    a. courage   b. confidence

    c. contempt

9. Oz told the Tin Woodman that a heart makes most people ▪▪▪ .

    a. unhappy   b. happy

    c. frightened

B CHARACTER TRAITS

Circle *true* or *false* for each statement about Oz.

1. Oz is a humbug.

    • true   • false

2. Oz lives in the Emerald City.

    • true   • false

3. Oz is a ball of fire.

    • true   • false

4. Oz is a little old man.

    • true   • false

5. Oz is a lovely lady.

    • true   • false

6. Oz is more powerful than the witches.

    • true   • false

7. Oz is a ventriloquist.

    • true   • false

C ⬛ SETTINGS

Complete each sentence with *forest,*
Throne Room,* or *Witch's Castle.

1. In the _____ ,
   the Lion saw a ball of fire.

2. In the _____ ,
   Dorothy threw a bucket of water
   at somebody.

3. In the _____ ,
   The Kalidahs attacked the travelers.

4. In the _____ ,
   Dorothy found a cap in a cupboard.

5. In the _____ ,
   Oz gave Dorothy a command.

D ⬛ SEQUENCING

**Number the events in the correct
sequence.**

_____ The Winged Monkeys took the
travelers to the Emerald City.

_____ Oz told the story of his life.

_____ Oz ordered the travelers to kill the
Wicked Witch.

_____ Dorothy tripped over an invisible
iron bar.

_____ Oz pretended to be a giant head.

E ⬛ VOCABULARY

**Complete each sentence with the
correct word.**

advanced	exclaim	promptly
cunning	feast	reunited
enormous	mend	tempt

1. Walt could never find shoes big enough to
   fit his _____ feet.

2. The army _____ slowly
   across the plain.

3. The splendid jewels he promised did not
   _____ her.

4. The witch was very cruel and
   _____ .

5. The people sat down at a table filled with
   food and prepared to have a
   _____ .

6. The friends rejoiced when they were
   _____ at last.

7. When the alarm rings, get up
   _____ .

GO TO PART C IN YOUR TEXTBOOK

A STORY DETAILS

Work the items.

1. What two types of metal objects did Oz put in the Scarecrow's head?

    _____

2. Those objects showed that the Scarecrow was very ▨ .

    a. brave   b. sharp

    c. kindhearted

3. Oz used shears to ▨ .

    a. cut a hole in the Tin Woodman

    b. make the Tin Woodman's heart

    c. polish the Tin Woodman

4. The Tin Woodman's heart was made of silk stuffed with _____ .

5. Oz told the Lion the liquid in the dish was ▨ .

    a. curdled   b. curry

    c. courage

6. Oz's old balloon was made of silk coated with _____ to keep the air from leaking out.

7. If the air inside a balloon is hot, the balloon will ▨ .

    a. fall   b. stand still   c. rise

8. If the air inside a balloon gets cold, the balloon will ▨ .

    a. fall   b. stand still   c. rise

B VOCABULARY

Complete each sentence with the correct word.

bald	humbug	overhear
experience	imitate	promptly
gradually	knowledge	ventriloquist

1. The wall was so thin that you could _____ what people were saying on the other side.

2. The slow turtle _____ moved around the pond.

3. The man was so _____ that he never got a haircut.

4. The _____ could throw her voice across the room.

5. Climbing the mountain was an unforgettable _____ .

6. The parrot could _____ what people said.

7. Some people think that Santa Claus is a _____ .

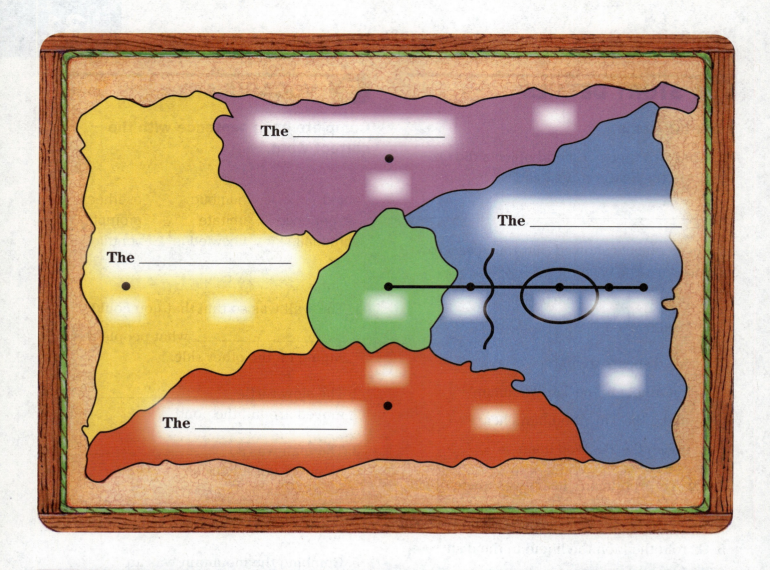

The _____

The _____

The _____

The _____

The _____

C   MAPS

Work the items.

1. On the map above, write the name of the people who live in each land.

2. Write **RS** on the lands that are closest to the rising sun.

3. Write **SS** on the lands that are closest to the setting sun.

4. Write **X** on the dot where Dorothy and Toto landed.

5. Write **S** on the dot where Dorothy met the Scarecrow.

6. Write **F** on the dot in the middle of the forest.

7. Write **R** next to the river.

8. Write **E** on the Emerald City.

9. Write **Y** on the dot where the Wicked Witch melted.

GO TO PART C IN YOUR TEXTBOOK

Name ______________________________

A STORY DETAILS

Work the items.

1. Oz filled the balloon with ______________ air.
2. Why did Dorothy go into the crowd while Oz was waiting for her?
   a. She wanted to say goodbye to the other travelers.
   b. She was afraid of riding in the balloon.
   c. She needed to find Toto.
3. What happened to the balloon while Dorothy was running toward it?
   a. It rose up in the air.
   b. It exploded.
   c. It began filling with hot air.
4. After Oz left, the Tin Woodman cried because he ______.
   a. was sad that Oz had left
   b. was sad that Dorothy couldn't go back to Kansas
   c. missed the Munchkin girl
5. When the travelers met in the throne room, the ______________ was sitting on the throne.
6. The character on the throne was now the ______ of the Emerald City.
   a. wizard
   b. ruler
   c. property
7. The name of the Witch of the South is ______________

B VOCABULARY

Complete each sentence with the correct word.

batter	preferred	reunited
desperately	promptly	slightest
feast	pure	tenderly

1. The boy drank water, but he ______________ milk.
2. Sheila ______________ held on to the rope as she swung in the air.
3. They were very full after their Thanksgiving ______________.
4. Sam had to handle the roses ______________, or they would fall apart.
5. Most of the time she arrived ______________, but sometimes she was late.
6. After being separated for many years, the brothers were ______________.
7. They melted the snow to make ______________ water.

C CHARACTER TRAITS

Complete each sentence with *North, South, East,* or *West.*

1. The Witch of the _____ made the Winkies her slaves.

2. The Witch of the _____ lived with the Gillikins.

3. The Witch of the _____ was killed by Dorothy's house.

4. The Witch of the _____ gave Dorothy a kiss.

5. The Witch of the _____ lived with the Quadlings.

6. The Witch of the _____ made the Munchkins her slaves.

7. The Witch of the _____ was the most powerful witch.

D CHARACTER STATEMENTS

Complete each sentence with *Dorothy, Glinda, The Lion, The Scarecrow,* or *The Woodman.*

1. _____ said, "I miss Oz so much that I think I'll cry."

2. _____ said, "Thanks to Oz, I am very sharp."

3. _____ said, "I am the most powerful witch."

4. _____ said, "City life does not agree with me."

5. _____ said, "I like it here, but I still want to go home."

6. _____ said, "I live on the edge of the desert."

E SETTINGS

Complete each sentence with *Field of Flowers, River,* or *Throne Room.*

1. In the _____ , you see a lovely lady with wings.

2. In the _____ , your raft gets carried away by the current.

3. In the _____ , you see a chair made of emeralds.

4. In the _____ , a strong smell puts you to sleep.

5. In the _____ , you see hundreds of plants with red blossoms.

GO TO PART C IN YOUR TEXTBOOK

Name _____

A STORY DETAILS

Work the items.

1. What color were houses in the Land of the South? _____

2. What gem was Glinda's throne made of? _____

3. Glinda will use the _____ _____ to command the Winged Monkeys.

4. After Dorothy leaves, the Scarecrow will go to the _____ .

5. After Dorothy leaves, the Tin Woodman will find the _____ maiden.

6. After Dorothy leaves, the Lion will go back to the _____ .

7. To make the silver shoes work, Dorothy first had to ▇ three times.
   a. twirl the golden cap
   b. jump up and down
   c. clap the heels together

8. Then Dorothy had to tell the silver shoes ▇ .
   a. where she wanted to go
   b. why she deserved a wish
   c. what she wanted to look like

9. Why didn't Dorothy have the silver shoes when she got back to Kansas?
   a. They fell off during her flight.
   b. They went back to the Land of Oz.
   c. They vanished into thin air.

B VOCABULARY

Complete each sentence with the correct word.

desperately	farewell	tint
dose	imitate	utter
extended	mischief	ventriloquist

1. When the zookeepers put the lion in a cage, it tried _____ to get out.

2. Those little puppies were full of _____ when they tore up the garden.

3. Janet was not a good _____ because you could see her mouth moving.

4. Martin could _____ the strange way the ducks walked.

5. To catch the ball, Ida _____ her arms as far as she could.

6. The shy boy didn't dare to _____ a word in class.

7. Domingo said _____ to all his friends before he moved away.

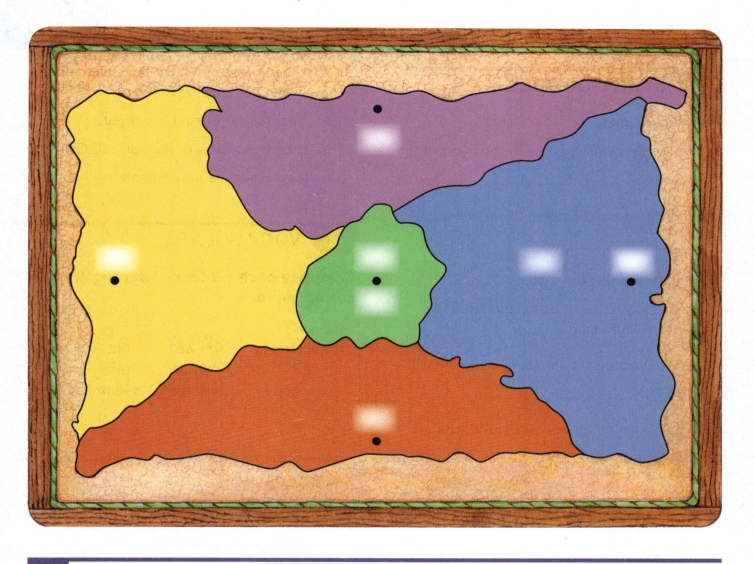

C MAPS

Work the items.

1. Write **X** on the dot where Dorothy's house landed.

2. Write **E** on the dot that shows the Emerald City.

3. Write **W** on the dot that shows the Wicked Witch's castle.

4. Write **G** on the dot that shows Glinda's castle.

5. Draw a straight line from **X** to **E**.

6. Draw a circle on the line to show where the forest is.

7. Draw a wavy line on the map to show where the river is.

8. Write **L** on the place where the Lion will live after Dorothy leaves.

9. Write **S** on the place where the Scarecrow will live after Dorothy leaves.

GO TO PART C IN YOUR TEXTBOOK

A STORY DETAILS

Langston Hughes lived in the _____ neighborhood of New York City.

a. Missouri   b. Harlem

c. Central Park

2. Mrs. Jones hit Roger _____
a. by mistake
b. _____
c. in his rear end

3. Mrs. Jones told Roger that his _____ was dirty.

a. shirt   b. hand   c. face

4. Who was at Roger's home?
a. nobody   b. his parents
c. his aunt

5. Why did Mrs. Jones say she wouldn't take Roger to jail?

Work the items.

b. He hadn't done anything wrong.
c. She would punish him herself.

6. Roger wanted a pair of blue _____ shoes.

7. Mrs. Jones told Roger, "Everybody's got something _____."

a. against me.   b. valuable

8. Mrs. Jones told Roger, "Shoes got by _____ ways will burn your feet.

a. legal   b. devilish   c. fiery

What couldn't Roger say to Mrs. Jones at _____
a. "The food was great."
b. "Give me more money."
c. "Thank you, m'am."

B VOCABULARY

_____ correct word.

| cocoa | presentable | stoop |
| latch | renaissance | suede |

1. The wrestler won the match when she put a half _____ on her opponent.

2. Hakeem's shoes were soft because they were made of _____ .

3. Elisa poured _____ powder into hot milk to make a chocolate drink.

4. Each _____ in the house had a kitchenette.

5. Forrest made himself _____ by combing his hair and washing his face.

6. The pickpocket tried to _____ onto Alonso's wallet.

9. Write **S** on the place where the Scarecrow

7. You have to climb up the _____ before you can enter the house.

C HYPHENS

- The first line in each item ends with a hyphenated word.

Write the complete word in the blank.

1. Nobody knows how Nell de-

    veloped her bad habit. _____

2. Mrs. Briggs worked for the tele-

    phone company. _____

3. Trains go on rail-

    road tracks. _____

4. The sheep were in the pas-

    ture next to the barn. _____

D CHARACTER STATEMENTS

Complete each sentence with *Roger* or *Mrs. Jones.*

1. _____ said, "Now ain't you ashamed of yourself?"

2. _____ said, "Yes'm."

3. _____ said, "I just want you to turn me loose."

4. _____ said, "I have done things, too, which I would not tell you."

5. _____ said, "Everybody's got something in common."

6. _____ couldn't even say, "Thank you, m'am."

E VOCABULARY IN CONTEXT

Circle the letter of the choice that means the same thing as the boldface word or phrase.

1. You can tell **they ain't** happy at the moment.

    a. they paint   b. they're not

    c. they can't be

2. Everyone cheered when the bat **came into contact with** the ball.

    a. touched   b. missed

    c. juggled

3. The nest was so **frail** that it blew apart in the wind.

    a. well built   b. delicate

    c. frozen

4. The **icebox** came with a built-in freezer.

    a. refrigerator   b. stove

    c. freezer

5. There was a **kitchenette** in a corner of the small room.

    a. large kitchen   b. tennis net

    c. small kitchen

6. You should **mistrust** someone who doesn't always tell the truth.

    a. believe in   b. not trust

    c. misguide

GO TO PART G IN YOUR TEXTBOOK

A VOCABULARY

Complete each sentence with the correct word.

chorus	deceive	region
confidence	disgusting	sunburnt
debris	gradually	whisk

1. Cats _____ their tails back and forth when they're angry.

2. You need real _____ to walk on a tightrope.

3. Those dirty socks smell _____ .

4. Every student in the class sang in a _____ .

5. The snail moved _____ across the garden.

6. It's hard to _____ someone who knows all the tricks.

7. The girl had to _____ the lost library book.

B HYPHENS

- The first line in each item ends with a hyphenated word.

Write the complete word in the blank.

1. The crowd of people approached the gate. _____

2. The driver checked the condition of the tires. _____

3. The flowers in the garden were blooming. _____

4. During the storm, lightning flashed across the sky.

   _____

C CHARACTER STATEMENTS

**Complete each sentence with *Dorothy,
The Lion, Oz, The Scarecrow,* or *The
Woodman.***

1. _____ said,
"I want to marry a Munchkin maiden."

2. _____ said,
"I want to be the King of Beasts."

3. _____ said,
"There is no place like home."

4. _____ said,
"I do not know where this balloon will
carry me."

5. _____ said,
"The Winged Monkeys will take me back
to the forest."

6. _____ said,
"The silver shoes carried me to Kansas."

7. _____ said,
"My brain is very sharp."

D SETTINGS

Write the color of each setting.

1. Land of the South _____

2. Land of the East _____

3. Land of the West _____

4. Field of Flowers _____

5. Emerald City _____

GO TO PART E IN YOUR TEXTBOOK

A STORY DETAILS

Work the items.

1. How many times had the mother duck laid eggs before?

   a. never   b. once   c. twice

2. The mother duck examined the eggs several times a day to see if the shells were _____ .

3. The neighbor duck thought the big egg was a _____ egg.

4. What hatched first, the little eggs or the big egg? _____

5. What color was the duckling who hatched first?

   _____

6. What color was the duckling who hatched last?

   _____

7. The ugly duckling was ▓▓▓ than the other ducklings.

   a. younger   b. bigger

   c. smaller

8. The loud duck said, "It certainly is a great shame that he is so _____ from the rest of us."

9. The ugly duckling became so sad that he decided to ▓▓▓ .

   a. fight the loud duck   b. run away

   c. stay in the nest all day

B CHARACTER STATEMENTS

Complete each sentence with *loud duck, mother duck,* or *ugly duckling*.

1. The _____ said, "This egg is a real problem."

2. The _____ said, "When you see the duckling by itself, it seems all right."

3. The _____ thought, "I don't fit in."

4. The _____ said, "It certainly is a great shame that he is so different from the rest of us."

5. The _____ said, "He is just so disgusting that I can't stand him!"

6. The _____ said, "When I compare it to the others, I can see how different it is."

7. The _____ thought, "I am tired of being picked on."

C VOCABULARY

Complete each sentence with the correct word.

bruise	echo	mistrust
debris	frail	mocked
ease	icebox	reeds

1. They could hear the _____ again and again as it faded away.

2. The clown _____ the other people in the circus.

3. Birds can fly through the air with _____ .

4. The river was lined with green _____ that swayed in the wind.

5. After he got tackled, the football player had a big _____ on his arm.

6. The bowl was too _____ to use for eating cereal.

7. The streets were filled with _____ from the flood.

D HYPHENS

- The first line in each item ends with a hyphenated word.

Write the complete word in the blank.

1. Losing a plane ticket can be a seri-ous problem. _____

2. The girls spent hours look-ing for their dog. _____

3. The fence was old and in bad condi-tion. _____

4. Everyone liked the wizard's mar-velous tricks. _____

GO TO PART E IN YOUR TEXTBOOK

A STORY DETAILS

Work the items.

1. In this chapter, the duckling first met a group of ▢ .

   a. ducks   b. swans   c. geese

2. The duckling wanted to stay with that group of birds forever because ▢ .

   a. They told him he was a young swan.

   b. They were going to stay in the reeds forever.

   c. They didn't tell him how ugly he was.

3. What happened to the two birds who asked the duckling to leave the plain with them?

   a. They were killed by a hunter.

   b. They froze to death during the winter.

   c. They turned into swans.

4. Why didn't the duckling fly away with the first group of birds?

   a. He wanted to stay in the reeds.

   b. He was too heavy to fly.

   c. He didn't know how to fly.

5. What direction were the swans flying before winter began?

   _____

6. The swans were flying to a place that was ▢ .

   a. colder   b. warmer

   c. the same

7. The pink blossoms the duckling saw covered an _____ tree.

8. The duckling discovered who he truly was by looking at his reflection in ▢ .

   a. a mirror   b. a window

   c. the water

B VOCABULARY

Complete each sentence with the correct word.

bill	contents	glorious
congratulated	disgusting	moss
considered	eventually	reflection

1. Carlo _____ reading the book, but it was very long.

2. The book had a table of

   _____ at the beginning.

3. After Dafna won the spelling contest, her classmates _____ her.

4. The rotting meat smelled

   _____ .

5. The rocks were green because they were covered with _____ .

6. The actor admired his

   _____ in the mirror.

7. The day seemed to last forever, but

   _____ the sun went down.

SEQUENCING

**Number the events in the
correct sequence.**

_____ The duckling discovered who he
really was.

_____ The duckling ran away from home.

_____ The duckling's brothers and sisters
were mean to him.

_____ The duckling stayed with some geese.

_____ The duckling almost froze to death.

GO TO PART D IN YOUR TEXTBOOK

A   STORY DETAILS

Work the items.

1. The world's fair in Chicago was called

   the _____ Exposition.

2. The fair displayed new inventions, such

   as _____ lights.

3. The fair organizers wanted something

   better than the _____
   Tower in Paris.

4. George's invention was called the

   _____ wheel.

5. The rims of the wheel revolved

   around an _____ .

6. The rims were attached to the center of

   the wheel with _____ .

7. In what year did the Chicago world's

   fair open? _____

8. At night, the wheel was lit by almost
   3,000 ▒▒▒ .

   a. gas lights   b. torches

   c. electric lights

B   VOCABULARY

**Complete each sentence with the
correct word.**

achievement	foundation
attractions	revolves
confirm	suspends
engineer	

1. Each year, the Earth _____
   once around the sun.

2. An electrical worker _____
   power lines between tall poles.

3. This bridge was designed by a well-known

   _____ .

4. The building _____ was
   made of concrete.

5. Inventing the Ferris wheel was the biggest

   _____ of George's life.

6. The Grand Canyon is one of the biggest

   _____ in the United States.

C | SEQUENCING

Number the events in the correct sequence.

_____ The rims were attached to the axle with spokes.

_____ Two towers were built on top of the foundations.

_____ Passenger cars were connected to the rims.

_____ An axle was suspended between the two towers.

_____ Concrete foundations were poured.

D | VOCABULARY REVIEW

Complete each sentence with the correct word.

bill	kitchenette
debris	region
eventually	sunburnt
glorious	

1. California is in the western

   _____ of the United States.

2. It took days to clean up the

   _____ from the house fire.

3. The family prepared their meals by using

   a small _____ .

4. The swan used its _____ to

   pick up food.

5. After the long winter, the first day of

   spring was _____ .

6. The race was long, but

   _____ everyone crossed

   the finish line.

GO TO PART E IN YOUR TEXTBOOK

A STORY DETAILS

Work the items.

1. In which country does "A Horse to Remember" take place?

    a. England   b. Scotland

    c. Wales

2. Near which city does the story take place?

    _____

3. Nellie's bad habit was ▩ fences.

    a. scratching   b. breaking

    c. jumping

4. What time of day was it when Tara first saw Nellie get out of the pasture?

    a. morning   b. afternoon

    c. night

5. Tara saw Nellie clearly because the sky was lit up by ▩ .

    a. the sun   b. lightning

    c. electric lights

6. Mr. Briggs tried to keep Nellie in the barn by ▩ .

    a. tying her up with a rope

    b. bolting her stall

    c. fixing the side door

7. Tara wanted to keep Nellie in the pasture by ▩ .

    a. electrifying the fence

    b. building a new barn

    c. making the fence higher

8. Mr. Briggs didn't approve of Tara's plan because it was too ▩ .

    a. expensive   b. risky

    c. impractical

B PICTURE CLUES

Work the items.

Horse 1   Horse 2

Horse 3   Horse 4

1. Which horse is Nellie?

    a. Horse 1   b. Horse 2

    c. Horse 3   d. Horse 4

2. Horse 1 is not Nellie because ▩ .

    a. she's the wrong color

    b. she's not swaybacked

    c. she has a long tail

3. Horse 3 is not Nellie because ▩ .

    a. she's the wrong color

    b. she's not swaybacked

    c. she has a long tail

C MAPS

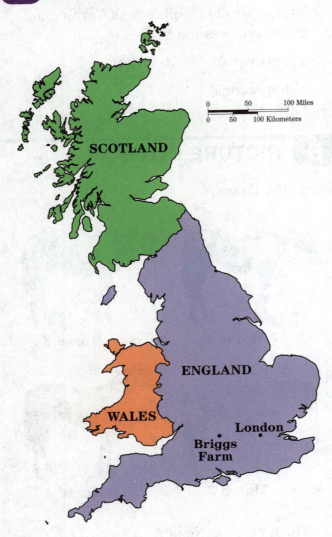

SCOTLAND

ENGLAND

WALES

London

Briggs
Farm

0   50   100 Miles
0   50   100 Kilometers

Work the items.

1. Draw an arrow from London to the Briggs farm.

2. In which direction does the arrow point from London to the Briggs farm?

_____

3. About how many miles is it from London to the farm?

_____

D VOCABULARY

Complete each sentence with the correct word.

alert	nag	plodded
confirm	nudge	revolve
develop	pasture	Thoroughbreds

1. The dog could _____ the door open with its nose.

2. A car's back tires _____ around its rear axle.

3. Some ranchers raise _____ for racing.

4. The _____ cat listened carefully for mice.

5. Cows _____ slowly down the muddy trail.

6. Every _____ on the farm was covered with tall grass.

7. Mr. Briggs checked the fence to _____ that it wasn't broken.

GO TO PART D IN YOUR TEXTBOOK

A | STORY DETAILS

Work the items.

1. When Tara woke up, there was a hint of light along the horizon to the

   _____ .

2. What time of day was that?

   a. dawn   b. dusk

   c. mid-morning

3. Tara used a _____ engine on the computer to find what she was looking for.

4. What was the first topic she searched for?

   a. steeplechase   b. Grand National

   c. jumping horses

5. What was the next topic she selected?

   a. steeplechase   b. Grand National

   c. jumping horses

6. Tara's mother suggested that she talk

   to Mr. _____ .

7. What kind of job did he have?

   a. blacksmith   b. gunsmith

   c. tinsmith

8. If Nellie proved she could jump, he said he would help ▮▮▮ her.

   a. shoe   b. groom   c. train

9. Nellie proved she could jump by jumping over a ▮▮▮ .

   a. pole   b. fence   c. ditch

B | RELATED FACTS

For each jump, write *fence*, *high jump*, *hedge*, *bank*, or *combined jump*.

1. _____ .

2. _____ .

3. _____ .

4. _____ .

C RELATED FACTS

Work the items.

1. A steeplechase is ▨ a regular horse race.

   a. shorter than

   b. the same length as

   c. longer than

2. Another way a steeplechase is different from a regular horse race is that horses in a steeplechase ▨ .

   a. pull carts

   b. jump over obstacles

   c. swim across rivers

3. Horses in steeplechases are ▨ Thoroughbreds.

   a. never   b. sometimes

   c. always

4. The most famous steeplechase is the ▨ .

   a. Grand National

   b. Grand Ole Opry

   c. Grand Central

D VOCABULARY

Complete each sentence with the correct word.

achievement	endurance	foundation
attraction	engineer	stall
barrier	exhausted	suspend

1. You need a lot of _____ to climb tall mountains.

2. The wooden barn was built on top of a concrete _____ .

3. The players were _____ after the long soccer game.

4. The Statue of Liberty is a big _____ for tourists in New York City.

5. Each cow had its own _____ in the barn.

GO TO PART E IN YOUR TEXTBOOK

Name ______________________________

A STORY DETAILS

Work the items.

1. Mr. Jones set up a training course for Nellie in a ____ behind his shop.
   a. forest   b. parking lot
   c. pasture

2. At first, the jumps were a little less than ____ feet high.
   a. three   b. four   c. five

3. Mr. Jones said he would raise the jumps when ____ .
   a. Nellie could go over them
   b. Tara could stay on Nellie
   c. Tara got good grades

4. At first, Tara fell off when Nellie was ____ .
   a. taking off
   b. halfway across the jump
   c. landing

5. Later, Tara fell off when Nellie was ____ .
   a. taking off
   b. halfway across the jump
   c. landing

6. Tara fell ____ when Nellie was taking off.
   a. backward   b. sideways
   c. forward

7. Tara fell ____ when Nellie was landing.
   a. backward   b. sideways
   c. forward

8. The mayor was angry because Mr. Jones didn't fix his ____ .
   a. horseshoes   b. tractor wheel
   c. iron gate

B VOCABULARY

Complete each sentence with the correct word.

abruptly	endurance	marveled
brace	exhausted	obstacle
dilapidated	gallop	spectators

1. Amina can keep on running because she has a great deal of ____________________ .
2. Most of the ____________________ at the baseball game wore baseball hats.
3. When you ride a horse over a fence, you need to ____________________ yourself for the landing.
4. The driver stopped ____________________ when she saw a child in the road.
5. The landslide was a giant ____________________ on the freeway.
6. The music teacher ____________________ at his student's piano playing.
7. The goats lived in a ____________________ old barn.

C DIAGRAMS

Write the answers on the picture.

1. Label the streambed.

2. Label the stream.

3. Label the left bank.

4. Label the right bank.

5. Write **first** on the arrow that shows Nellie's first jump with Tara.

6. Write **second** on the arrow that shows Nellie's second jump with Tara.

D RELATED FACTS

Work the items.

1. This rider is not braced for a takeoff. Draw an arrow to show which way the rider will fall.

2. This rider is not braced for a landing. Draw an arrow to show which way the rider will fall.

GO TO PART E IN YOUR TEXTBOOK

A STORY DETAILS

Work the items.

1. When the race began, Nellie .

   a. threw Tara to the ground

   b. took the lead

   c. refused to start

2. Tara held on to the ▨▨ to prevent Nellie from running away.

   a. rains   b. reigns   c. reins

3. When Nellie started running, Tara ▨▨ .

   a. let Nellie go at full speed

   b. didn't let Nellie go at full speed

   c. told Nellie to walk

4. Nellie and the mayor's horse started a ▨▨ jump at the same time.

   a. combined   b. hedge   c. bank

5. What did Nellie do at that jump?

   a. cleared the obstacle with ease

   b. landed in the obstacle

   c. went around the obstacle

6. What did the mayor's horse do?

   a. cleared the obstacle with ease

   b. landed in the obstacle

   c. went around the obstacle

7. Which horse was leading the race at the end of the chapter?

   a. Nellie   b. the mayor's horse

   c. the black horse

B VOCABULARY

Complete each sentence with the correct word.

ability	encouragement	official
applaud	mount	shabby
circular	numb	triangular

1. The racetrack was like a circle, so it was

   _____ .

2. Nora could feel the dentist's drill even though her mouth was

   _____ .

3. Niran liked to wear _____ old clothes on the weekend.

4. Cats have the _____ to jump high in the air.

5. One kind of _____ is a referee.

6. The spectators started to

   _____ even before the song was over.

7. People usually _____ a horse from the left side.

C MAPS

Work the items.

County Racetrack

1. Number the jumps in order from **1** to **5.**

2. Write **X** above the starting line.

3. Write the type of jump for each location.

- Jump 1: _____
- Jump 2: _____
- Jump 3: _____
- Jump 4: _____
- Jump 5: _____

D RELATED FACTS

Complete each sentence with the correct number.

1. The course at the county racetrack is

_____ mile around.

2. The horses go around the racetrack

_____ times.

3. The horses must run _____ miles to finish the entire race.

4. The racetrack has _____ jumps.

5. The horses must make

_____ jumps to finish the race.

GO TO PART D IN YOUR TEXTBOOK

A STORY DETAILS

Work the items.

1. At the beginning of the chapter, what did Mr. Jones yell above the roaring crowd?

   a. Hold her in, Tara!

   b. Let her out, Tara!

   c. Don't push her too hard!

2. Which horse was the first to cross the finish line?

   a. Nellie   b. Nighthawk

   c. The mayor's horse

3. That horse lost the race because it ▨▨▨ .

   a. missed a jump   b. lost its saddle

   c. didn't have a rider

4. Who was waiting for Tara and the others at Mr. Jones's blacksmith shop?

   a. Mr. Longly   b. the mayor

   c. Mr. Briggs

5. What did that person want to buy?

   _____

6. He offered to pay

   _____ pounds.

7. Which member of the Briggs family was thinking about selling Nellie?

   _____

8. Who convinced that person not to sell Nellie?

   _____

B RELATED FACTS

Write the name of each jump.

1. _____

2. _____

3. _____

4. _____

C MAPS

Work the items.

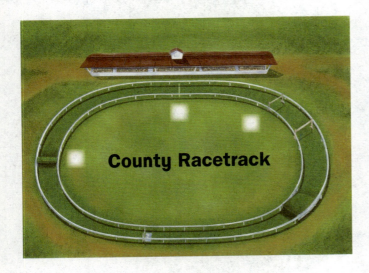

County Racetrack

1. Write **X** on the place where Nellie threw Tara.

2. Write **Y** on the place where Tara let Nellie out.

3. Write **Z** on the place where the black horse threw its rider.

D SETTINGS

Complete each sentence with *the East, the Emerald City, Kansas,* or *the West.*

1. Dorothy saw gray prairies in

   _____.

2. Dorothy saw blue fences in the Land of

   _____.

3. Dorothy saw walls studded with green jewels in

   _____.

4. Dorothy saw a yellow castle in the Land of

   _____.

E RELATED FACTS

Complete each sentence with the correct number.

1. The course at the county racetrack is

   _____ mile around.

2. The horses go around the racetrack

   _____ times.

3. The horses must run _____ miles to finish the entire race.

4. The racetrack has _____ jumps.

5. The horses must make _____ jumps to finish the race.

GO TO PART E IN YOUR TEXTBOOK

A STORY DETAILS

Work the items.

1. How many steeplechases had Nellie won when she entered the Grand National?

   _____

2. Nellie lost one steeplechase because she ▨ .

   a. missed a jump

   b. came in after another horse

   c. threw Tara

3. Mr. Longly didn't think Nellie had enough ▨ to win the Grand National.

   a. speed   b. endurance

   c. weight

4. Near the end of the county race, Nighthawk's rider was ▨ .

   a. holding him in   b. letting him out

   c. out of the saddle

5. About how many horses entered the Grand National?

   a. twenty   b. thirty   c. forty

6. Nellie's number was _____ .

7. Which two horses were next to Nellie?

   a. Nighthawk and the mayor's horse

   b. the mayor's horse and the Arabian horse

   c. the Arabian horse and Nighthawk

8. What color was Tara's jacket?

   _____

B VOCABULARY

Complete each sentence with the correct word.

cautioned	lag	prancing
dangled	magnificent	strain
frantically	pounds	turf

1. The grass and soil in the _____ were held together by the roots of the grass.

2. Prakash started out quickly, but he soon began to _____ behind the other runners.

3. These shirts cost twenty _____ each at a store in London, England.

4. The nervous horse began _____ around with high steps.

5. A gold necklace _____ around Reta's neck.

6. People in the burning house tried _____ to escape.

7. The teacher _____ the students about tricky questions on the test.

C MAPS

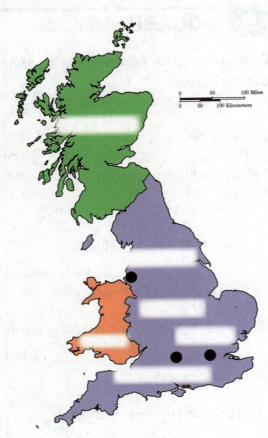

Work the items.

1. Write the correct name on each country.

   • England

   • Scotland

   • Wales

2. Write the correct name next to each dot.

   • Briggs Farm

   • Liverpool

   • London

3. What is the main direction you travel to get from Liverpool to the Briggs farm?

   a. north   b. south

   c. east   d. west

D RELATED FACTS

Work the items.

1. About how far around is the racetrack at the Grand National?

   a. one mile   b. two miles

   c. four miles

2. How many times do the horses go around the Grand National track?

   a. one time   b. two times

   c. four times

3. How many jumps do the horses make to finish the race?

   a. 14   b. 16   c. 30

4. The shape of the track at the Grand National is ▓▓▓ .

   a. rectangular   b. triangular

   c. circular

5. The shape of the county track was ▓▓▓ .

   a. rectangular   b. triangular

   c. circular

6. The rider is not braced. In which direction will she fall?

   a. forward   b. backward

   c. sideways

GO TO PART D IN YOUR TEXTBOOK

A STORY DETAILS

Work the items.

1. Mr. Jones told Tara to hold Nellie in until there were only ▮▮▮ jumps left in the race.

   a. one or two   b. three or four

   c. five or six

2. Which horse matched Nellie stride for stride at the beginning of the race?

   _____

3. Right after Nighthawk started pulling away, Tara ▮▮▮ .

   a. held Nellie at an easy run

   b. pulled Nellie back

   c. let Nellie out

4. After Nellie cleared the twenty-sixth jump, Tara ▮▮▮ .

   a. held her at an easy run

   b. pulled her back

   c. let her out

5. Which was the last jump the horses went over together?

   a. 27th   b. 28th   c. 29th

6. Which horse landed ahead at that jump?

   _____

7. The announcer said that Nellie ▮▮▮ track record.

   a. had tied the   b. was close to the

   c. set a new

B VOCABULARY

Complete each sentence with the correct word.

ability	emperor	officials
applaud	encouraged	retire
continent	numb	shabby

1. All the kings bowed down to the

   _____ .

2. Austria is a country in the

   _____ of Europe.

3. The carpenter was getting old, so she

   decided to _____ .

4. A good singer has the _____ to hold a note for a long time.

5. The crowd _____ their team by cheering.

6. The soccer league used _____ to make sure everyone followed the rules.

C RELATED FACTS

Work the items.

1. The track at the Grand National is about ▮▮▮ miles around.

   a. two   b. three   c. four

2. How many times do the horses go around the track during the Grand National?

   a. one time   b. two times

   c. three times

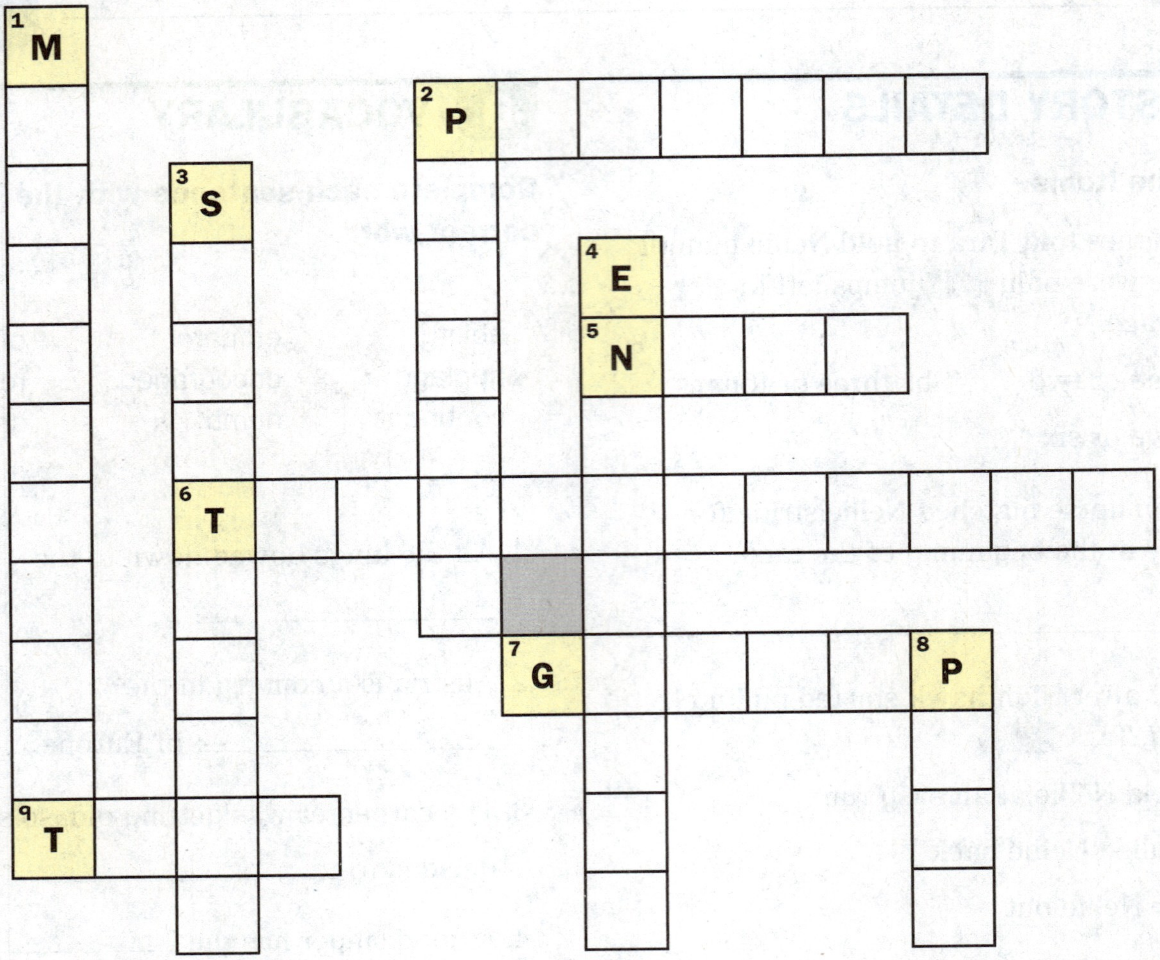

D CROSSWORD PUZZLE

Use the clues to complete the puzzle in CAPITAL LETTERS.

ACROSS

2. When a horse steps high in the air, it ____ .
5. When you have no feeling in a part of your body, that part is ____ .
6. A special breed of horse that is used for racing is a ____ .
7. When horses run very quickly, they ____ .
9. Grass and the soil underneath the grass is called ____ .

DOWN

1. Another word for *wonderful* or *marvelous* is ____ .
2. A field for farm animals is called a ____ .
3. People who watch an event are ____ .
4. A horse that can keep on going and going has a lot of ____ .
8. When you move at a very slow, tired pace, you ____ .

GO TO PART D IN YOUR TEXTBOOK

Name _____

A STORY DETAILS

Work the items.

1. Mozart was born in the continent of ▨ .
   a. North America   b. Asia
   c. Europe   d. Australia

2. Mozart was born in the country of ▨ .
   a. Germany   b. England
   c. Wales   d. Austria

3. Mozart was born in the city of ▨ .
   a. Salzburg   b. London
   c. Vienna

4. Which type of music has been around for more than a thousand years?
   a. hip hop   b. classical   c. rock

5. In which century was Mozart born?
   a. 1700s   b. 1800s   c. 1900s

6. Which type of classical piece features the orchestra by itself?
   a. concerto   b. opera
   c. symphony

7. Which type of classical piece uses songs to tell a story?
   a. concerto   b. opera
   c. symphony

8. During the last 10 years of his life, Mozart lived in the city of _____ .

9. How old was Mozart when he died?
   a. 25   b. 35   c. 45

10. The last piece of music Mozart wrote was for ▨ .
    a. a concerto   b. a funeral
    c. an opera   d. a ballet

B VOCABULARY

Complete each sentence with the correct word.

classical	opera	prodigy
composer	orchestra	salary
concerto	outstanding	symphony

1. A piece of classical music is written by a _____ .

2. Melinda won first place because she was _____ .

3. In a _____ , one or more musicians play in front of the orchestra.

4. Vinjay was poor because he earned a low _____ .

5. The child _____ astonished the audience with her violin playing.

6. The _____ we saw was a play that used music to tell a story.

7. The _____ we heard was a long classical piece that featured an orchestra by itself.

C MAIN IDEA

Write the main idea for each picture or row of pictures.

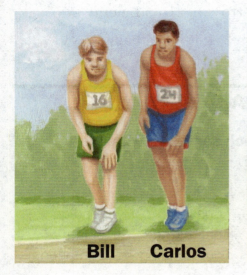
Bill   Carlos

1. _____

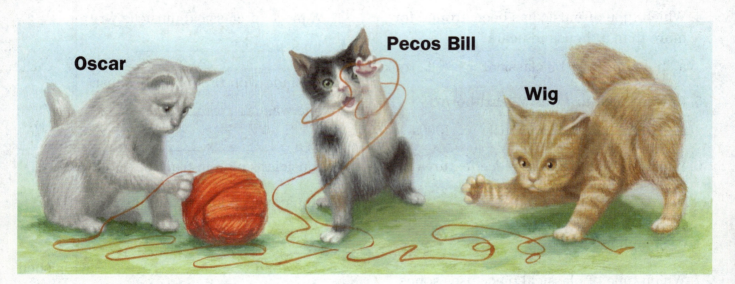
Oscar   Pecos Bill   Wig

2. _____

GO TO PART E IN YOUR TEXTBOOK

Name _____

A STORY DETAILS

Work the items.

1. _____ animals don't live with people.

2. _____ animals do live with people.

3. The wild _____ was probably the first animal to become domesticated.

4. That animal was domesticated ▮ of years ago.

   a. hundreds   b. thousands

   c. millions

5. Which animal below would be the easiest to domesticate?

   a. young wild puppy

   b. older wild puppy

   c. full-grown wild dog

6. Wild dogs liked to live with people because people ▮ .

   a. kept them hungry

   b. ignored them

   c. gave them food

7. Wild dogs could help people ▮ .

   a. grow food

   b. hunt wild animals

   c. build houses

8. Who got more use out of domestic goats?

   a. dogs   b. farmers   c. hunters

9. Name a product people got from goats.

   a. pork   b. bread   c. milk

B VOCABULARY

Complete each sentence with the correct word.

advantages	outstanding	relatives
generation	prey	retire
keen	prodigy	salary

1. An animal that is hunted by another animal is called _____ .

2. Your _____ are the people who are part of your family.

3. The _____ of a plan are the ways the plan is better than another plan.

4. A _____ is a young person who has outstanding talent.

5. A _____ is the amount of money workers get paid for their jobs.

6. A _____ is a group of people who grow up at the same time.

7. If you have _____ hearing, your hearing is very good.

C SETTINGS

Complete each sentence with *the Briggs farm, the county racetrack, Liverpool,* or *London.*

1. Nellie won her first race at

_____ .

2. The Grand National was held near

_____ .

3. The race course at

_____

is circular.

4. Nellie lived at

_____ .

5. The race course near

_____

is triangular.

D SEQUENCING

Number the events in the correct sequence.

____ Nellie won the race at Liverpool.

____ Tara found out about Nellie's bad habit.

____ Nellie won the race at the county racetrack.

____ Mr. Jones agreed to train Nellie.

____ Nellie had a colt.

E CLASSIFICATION

Complete each sentence with *domestic* or *wild.*

1. Tigers are _____ animals.

2. Pigs are _____ animals.

3. Dogs are _____ animals.

4. Alligators are _____ animals.

5. Chickens are _____ animals.

6. Sheep are _____ animals.

7. Lions are _____ animals.

GO TO PART D IN YOUR TEXTBOOK

A STORY DETAILS

Work the items.

1. Wild _____ were probably the first animal to be domesticated.

2. What was the main use for that animal?

   a. carrying   b. milking

   c. hunting

3. Which country domesticated an animal to help with its grain problem?

   _____

4. What problem did that country have with its grain?

   a. The grain was rotting.

   b. Mice and rats were eating the grain.

   c. They didn't grow enough grain.

5. Which animals solved that problem?

   a. cats   b. dogs   c. falcons

6. Which animals do mongooses attack?

   a. cobars   b. cobras   c. corbas

7. The claws of a falcon are called ▯ .

   a. tendons   b. talents   c. talons

8. The _____ is a South American animal that is good at climbing mountains.

B CLASSIFICATION

Complete each sentence with *hunting*, *food*, or *carrying things*.

1. People use cats for

   _____ .

2. People use camels for

   _____ .

3. People use mongooses for

   _____ .

4. People use elephants for

   _____ .

5. People use goats for

   _____ .

6. People use llamas for

   _____ .

7. People use chickens for

   _____ .

8. People use cheetahs for

   _____ .

C | CLASSIFICATION

**Complete each sentence with *eggs*,
leather, *wool*, or *meat*. Fill in both blanks
in each sentence.**

1. Cows produce _____

   and _____ .

2. Chickens produce _____

   and _____ .

3. Sheep produce _____

   and _____ .

4. Pigs produce _____

   and _____ .

D | RELATED FACTS

**Pretend that a farmer wants larger
chicken eggs.**

1. The farmer would keep breeding the
   chickens that laid ▓▓ eggs.

   a. small   b. normal   c. big

2. After many generations, the new chickens
   would lay ▓▓ eggs.

   a. smaller   b. normal   c. bigger

E | VOCABULARY

**Complete each sentence with the
correct word.**

classical	opera
composer	orchestra
concerto	symphony

1. A long piece of music that features
   the orchestra by itself is called a

   _____ .

2. The type of music that Mozart wrote is

   called _____ music.

3. The _____ is a type of play
   that uses music to tell a story.

4. The violinist stood in front of the

   orchestra to play a _____ .

5. Someone who writes music is called

   a _____ .

GO TO PART C IN YOUR TEXTBOOK

Name ______________________________________

A STORY DETAILS

Work the items.

1. The man and the woman made a ________________ that gave off light.

2. The woman gave the wild dog a roasted ________________ bone.

3. The woman asked the dog to help the man ________________ in the daytime.

4. The woman asked the dog to ________________ the cave at night.

5. Which animal came to the cave first?
   a. wild cow
   b. wild horse
   c. wild dog

6. What name did the woman give that animal?
   a. First Friend
   b. First Servant
   c. Giver of Good Food

7. Which two animals liked the smell of the dried grass?
   a. wild dog and wild horse
   b. wild horse and wild cow
   c. wild cow and wild cat

8. The woman asked one of the animals to wear a ________________ .

9. That animal will help the man and the woman by ______ .
   a. giving them milk
   b. carrying them
   c. guarding them

B CHARACTER STATEMENTS

Complete each sentence with *woman, cat, cow, dog,* or *horse.*

1. The ________________ said, "I will give you this grass if you will be our servant."

2. The ________________ said, "That woman is wise, but she is not as wise as I am."

3. The ________________ said, "I will wear that collar."

4. The ________________ said, "I will give you this bone if you will guard our cave."

5. The ________________ said, "I walk by myself, no matter where I go."

6. The ________________ said, "I will give you this grass if you will give me your milk."

7. The ________________ said, "I will help you hunt."

C VOCABULARY

Complete each sentence with the correct word.

advantages	gnaw	prey
bargain	keen	relative
generation	pounce	shall

1. Children and their parents are not from the same _____ .

2. The lion crouched and waited for its _____ to come closer.

3. The lion is a _____ of the house cat.

4. Some people like to _____ on chicken bones.

5. The people sang, "We _____ overcome."

6. The wild dog made a poor _____ with the woman.

7. The woman said, "Living in a cave has many _____ ."

D CLASSIFICATION

Complete each sentence with *milking, selling, carrying,* or *hunting.*

1. The cave people used the dog for _____ .

2. The cave people used the cow for _____ .

3. The cave people used the horse for _____ .

E FACT AND FANTASY

Write whether each event is *fact* or *fantasy*.

1. The dog was the first animal to be domesticated. _____

2. It took only a couple of minutes to domesticate the dog. _____

3. People lived in caves. _____

4. The horse carried things for people. _____

5. The cow was domesticated one day after the dog was domesticated. _____

6. The animals spoke English to each other and to people. _____

GO TO PART E IN YOUR TEXTBOOK

Name _____

A STORY DETAILS

Work the items.

1. At first, the woman told the cat that she had all the ▨ she needed.

   a. friends and servants

   b. boys and girls

   c. milk and grass

2. The cat told the woman that she was ▨ .

   a. young and pretty

   b. mean and ugly

   c. wise and beautiful

3. The ▨ told the cat about the baby.

   a. bat   b. woman   c. dog

4. The woman praised the cat the first time because he ▨ the baby.

   a. protected   b. entertained

   c. captured

5. After the woman praised the cat once, he got to sit ▨ of the cave.

   a. at the front   b. in the middle

   c. at the back

6. The woman praised the cat the second time because he ▨ .

   a. caught a mouse

   b. helped the baby sleep

   c. talked to the bat

7. After the woman praised the cat twice, he got to sit ▨ of the cave.

   a. at the front   b. in the middle

   c. at the back

8. The woman praised the cat the third time because he ▨ .

   a. played with a ball of thread

   b. helped the baby sleep

   c. caught a mouse

9. After the woman praised the cat three times, he got to ▨ .

   a. drink the milk

   b. sit at the back of the cave

   c. play with the mouse

B SEQUENCING

Number the events in the correct sequence.

_____ The cat got to sit near the mouth of the cave.

_____ The woman and the cat made a bargain.

_____ The cat got to drink the milk.

_____ The cat got to sit next to the fire.

Copyright © McGraw-Hill Education

Lesson 50   99

C CHARACTER STATEMENTS

Complete each sentence with *cat*, *woman*, or *dog*.

1. The _____ said, "I am not a friend, and I am not a servant."

2. The _____ said, "If I praise you, you may sit in the cave."

3. The _____ said, "I am too busy cooking to deal with the baby."

4. The _____ said, "I still walk by myself."

5. The _____ said, "I must keep quiet, or I will praise him again."

6. The _____ said, "You are very wise and very beautiful."

7. The _____ said, "We do not need any more friends or servants."

D VOCABULARY

Complete each sentence with the correct word.

abnormal	environment	pounced
access	facilities	shall
bargain	gnaw	

1. After making the _____ , the women shook hands.

2. The cat _____ on the mouse in a flash.

3. Dogs like to _____ on bones.

4. When you are able to get something, you have _____ to it.

5. It is _____ to eat with your feet.

6. The _____ near the ocean is wet and windy.

7. Power plants are special _____ for making electricity.

GO TO PART D IN YOUR TEXTBOOK

A STORY DETAILS

Work the items.

1. The front teeth of a horse are called ▩ .

   a. canines   b. incisors   c. molars

2. The back teeth of a horse are called ▩ .

   a. canines   b. incisors   c. molars

3. A wild horse's teeth wear down evenly because the horse eats ▩ foods.

   a. soft   b. gritty   c. cooked

4. Wild horses have ▩ to food at all times.

   a. access   b. abscess   c. excess

5. When a horse grinds its food, the lower jaw moves in an ▩ motion.

   a. opal   b. oral   c. oval

6. Horses need good ▩ between their molars to grind food properly.

   a. contact   b. context

   c. contracts

7. The most important thing during a dental exam is to keep the horse's head ▩ .

   a. moving   b. still   c. neighing

8. The tool most commonly used by horse dentists is a ▩ .

   a. drill   b. sander   c. hand file

9. Hooks, ramps, waves, and points are ▩ tooth conditions for a horse.

   a. normal   b. abnormal

   c. paranormal

B MAIN IDEA

Write the main idea for each passage.

1. Some balloons can cross the ocean.
   Some sailboats can cross the ocean.
   Some planes can cross the ocean.

   _____

   _____

2. Angela liked to play baseball.
   Angela liked to play hockey.
   Angela liked to play basketball.

   _____

   _____

3. The hound dog could track the scent of wild rabbits.
   The hound dog could track the scent of wild pigs.
   The hound dog could track the scent of wild foxes.

   _____

   _____

4. The maples in the park were beautiful.
   The oaks in the park were beautiful.
   The pines in the park were beautiful.

   _____

   _____

C VOCABULARY

Complete each sentence with the correct word.

abnormal	facilities	instinct
access	grit	oval
environment	infected	permanent

1. Something that is not normal is

   _____ .

2. Loose bits of stone and sand are called

   _____ .

3. Wild horses have _____ to natural food at all times.

4. A behavior that animals don't learn is

   called an _____ .

5. Places that are designed for cooking are

   called kitchen _____ .

6. A cut that is _____ becomes swollen and painful.

7. After you lose your baby teeth, you get

   _____ teeth.

D TYPES OF READING MATERIAL

Complete each sentence with *factual*, *fantasy*, or *realistic fiction*.

1. Reading material that tells about facts is

   _____ .

2. Stories that are far from fact are called

   _____ .

3. Stories that are close to facts are called

   _____ .

4. "The Cat that Walked by Himself" is

   _____ .

5. "The Domestication of Animals" is

   _____ .

6. "A Horse to Remember" is

   _____ .

GO TO PART D IN YOUR TEXTBOOK

A STORY DETAILS

Work the items.

1. Write **S** next to forces that make slow changes in the landscape. Write **F** next to forces that make fast changes in the landscape.

   _____ hurricanes

   _____ wind

   _____ volcanic eruptions

   _____ landslides

   _____ snow

   _____ ice

   _____ earthquakes

2. Rivers carry mud, stones, and rocks from _____ places to _____ places.

3. What carries stones in the ocean?

   a. wind   b. rivers   c. waves

4. After millions of years, the ocean turns rocks into tiny grains of _____ .

5. Hot melted rock that comes from volcanoes is called _____ .

6. Events that split the earth are called _____ .

7. Heavy rains can trigger ▓▓ in hilly areas.

   a. hurricanes   b. landslides

   c. earthquakes

8. The soil in hilly areas is kept in place by the _____ of trees and plants.

9. Wetlands can ▓▓ the wall of water from a hurricane.

   a. observe   b. repel   c. absorb

10. Sand dunes and wetlands can prevent unnecessary _____ .

B TYPES OF READING MATERIAL

Complete each sentence with *factual*, *fantasy*, or *realistic fiction*.

1. *The Wizard of Oz* is

   _____ .

2. The Mozart biography is

   _____ .

3. "Thank You, M'am" is

   _____ .

4. "The Ugly Duckling" is

   _____ .

5. "What Big Teeth" is

   _____ .

C | VOCABULARY

Complete each sentence with the correct word.

absorbs	restore
hazard	seawall
landslide	sediment
lava	

1. When you repair something to make it look like new, you _____ it.

2. A _____ occurs when large amounts of mud and rock slide down from a hill or a mountain.

3. Small pieces of rock and sand that settle at the bottom of a river, lake, or ocean are called _____ .

4. Something that is dangerous is called a _____ .

5. When a sponge soaks up water, the sponge _____ the water.

6. An object that protects harbors from giant waves is called a _____ .

D | VOCABULARY REVIEW

abnormal	facilities	instinct
access	grit	oval
environment	infected	sedative

1. After the vet gave the dog a _____ , the dog felt relaxed and sleepy.

2. The doctor could tell the cut was _____ because the cut was swollen and painful.

3. An egg has an _____ shape.

4. Something that is not normal is called _____ .

5. Cats have a strong _____ to hunt.

6. Cities have a crowded and noisy _____ .

7. Wild pigs eat wild food that has a lot of _____ in it.

8. Mechanics work on cars in repair _____ .

GO TO PART E IN YOUR TEXTBOOK

Name ____ **53**

A STORY DETAILS

Work the items.

1. In what year was gold discovered in northern Canada?

   a. 1996   b. 1796   c. 1896

2. Near which town was the gold discovered?

   a. Dawson   b. Skagway

   c. Alaska

3. Your journey begins in the state of

   ____________________ .

4. You climb mountains until you reach ____ Lake.

   a. Bennett   b. Benton

   c. Breton

5. The lake is in the country of

   ____________________ .

6. From the lake, you go down the ____ River to reach your destination.

   a. Klondike   b. Yukon

   c. Noyuk

7. Your delight changes to ____ when you start down the river.

   a. happiness   b. despair

   c. fright

8. When you reach your destination, you will look for gold along the ____ River.

   a. Klondike   b. Yukon   c. Noyuk

B VOCABULARY

Complete each sentence with the correct word.

coil	hurl	sloshing
exchange	lean	treacherous
flicker		

1. People who have very little fat on their bodies are ____________________ .

2. The sailor wound the rope into a large ____________________ on the dock.

3. Something that is very dangerous is ____________________ .

4. They had a contest to see who could ____________________ the baseball the farthest.

5. The candle began to ____________________ in the wind.

6. Hiroshi drank so much water that he could feel the water ____________________ around in his stomach.

C FACT AND FANTASY

Write whether each item is *fact* or *fantasy.*

1. Kansas has tornadoes.

   _____

2. Tornadoes carry houses to the Land of Oz.

   _____

3. Scarecrows can speak and think.

   _____

4. Balloons filled with hot air can rise into

   the sky. _____

5. Scarecrows are stuffed with straw.

   _____

D CLASSIFICATION

Complete each sentence with *hunting, food,* or *carrying.*

1. Donkeys are used for

   _____ .

2. Cows are used for _____ .

3. Cats are used for _____ .

4. Camels are used for _____ .

5. Mongooses are used for

   _____ .

E VOCABULARY REVIEW

Complete each sentence with the correct word.

absorb	landslide	seawall
erupt	lava	sediment
hazard	restore	

1. The company tried to _____ the oil spill with straw.

2. Everyone was afraid that the volcano would _____ and destroy the town.

3. There were several feet of _____ at the bottom of the lake.

4. Ice on the road is a real _____ for drivers.

5. It took a long time to _____ the painting to its original condition.

6. They could see the _____ bubbling up from the volcano.

7. It was difficult to build the _____ in the stormy ocean.

GO TO PART E IN YOUR TEXTBOOK

A STORY DETAILS

Work the items.

1. The season at the beginning of the story

   was early _____ .

2. What town were the men on the sled
   trying to reach?

   _____

3. Their sled dogs were in ▮▮▮ condition.

   a. good   b. fair   c. poor

4. Thornton warned the men that the ice in
   the river might ▮▮▮ .

   a. collapse   b. harden

   c. be bumpy

5. What command did the driver give
   to the dogs when he wanted them to
   move forward?

   a. Gee!   b. Haw!   c. Mush on!

6. When the dogs did not follow the driver's
   command, he started ▮▮▮ them.

   a. petting   b. whipping

   c. kicking

7. Buck ▮▮▮ to follow the driver's command.

   a. decided   b. was eager

   c. refused

8. Thornton cut Buck's ▮▮▮ with the
   driver's knife.

   a. nails   b. harness   c. collar

9. After the drivers left Thornton's camp,
   they ▮▮▮ the ice.

   a. fell through   b. got stuck to

   c. tripped on

B VOCABULARY

**Complete each sentence with the
correct word.**

buds	murmur	stagger
Gee	runners	whittle
linger	sap	

1. The long strips of metal under a sled are

   called _____ .

2. Objects that turn into leaves are called

   _____ .

3. When you carve a piece of wood, you

   _____ it.

4. The dogs turned right when the driver

   said, " _____ !"

5. The liquid underneath the bark of a tree

   is called _____ .

6. Everybody else left the party, but Jordi

   decided to _____ on.

7. The dogs were so weak that they could

   only _____ along the trail.

C RELATED FACTS

Work the items.

1. Which direction is the dog turning?

   _____

2. Which command did the driver give?

   _____

3. Which direction is the dog turning?

   _____

4. Which command did the driver give?

   _____

D CHARACTER TRAITS

Complete each sentence with *Buck, The driver,* or *Thornton.*

1. _____ said, "I'll beat any dog that doesn't obey me."

2. _____ said, "This fool will not follow my advice."

3. _____ said, "I cannot stand to see that dog suffer."

4. _____ had felt the thin ice under his feet all day.

5. _____ said, "I'll make it to Dawson."

6. _____ had made up his mind not to get up.

GO TO PART F IN YOUR TEXTBOOK

A STORY DETAILS

Work the items.

1. Hans and Pete were Thornton's ▨ .
   a. brothers   b. partners
   c. enemies

2. Hans and Pete left Thornton in the tent so he could recover from ▨ .
   a. frozen feet   b. the flu
   c. fight injuries

3. Buck showed his love for Thornton by ▨ Thornton's hand.
   a. seizing   b. licking
   c. rubbing against

4. Buck acted ▨ toward people other than Thornton.
   a. warmly   b. fearfully
   c. coldly

5. When Thornton, Hans, and Pete were near a cliff, Thornton commanded Buck to jump ▨ .
   a. into his arms   b. over the cliff
   c. high in the air

6. Why couldn't Buck follow that command?
   a. The men held him back.
   b. He didn't understand the command.
   c. He was too afraid.

7. Thornton, Hans, and Pete traveled to Dawson on a ▨ .
   a. sled   b. train   c. raft

8. Why did Thornton step between two men in Dawson?
   a. To help one man stand up.
   b. To give them some advice.
   c. To stop them from fighting.

9. Why did Buck attack one of the men?
   a. The man hit Thornton.
   b. The man pulled a gun.
   c. The man was choking Thornton.

B VOCABULARY

Complete each sentence with the correct word.

embrace   ideal   recover
grapple   naked   tolerate
haunts

1. When something bothers you over and over, it _____ you.

2. When something is without covering, it is _____ .

3. When you hug somebody, you _____ them.

4. When you put up with something, you _____ it.

5. When you fight without weapons, you _____ .

6. When something is perfect, it is _____ .

C | MAPS

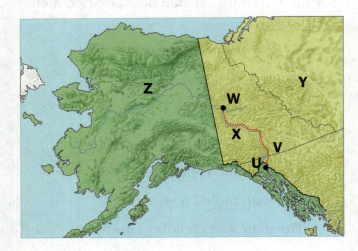

Write the name of each place.

1. Town **W** _____

2. State **Z** _____

3. Town **U** _____

4. Lake **V** _____

5. Country **Y** _____

6. River **X** _____

D | CHARACTER TRAITS

Complete each sentence with *Buck*, *Thornton*, or *Hans*.

1. _____ had frozen his feet.

2. _____ went up the Yukon to build a raft.

3. _____ would do anything for his master.

4. _____ was not a close friend of the dog's.

5. _____ gently bit someone's hand.

E | VOCABULARY REVIEW

Complete each sentence with the correct word.

buds	murmur	staggered
Gee!	runners	whittled
linger	sap	

1. It was so cold that the sled _____ froze to the ice.

2. The artist _____ a statue out of a block of wood.

3. They could see leaves coming out of the tree's _____ .

4. The frogs began to _____ and then to croak.

5. The _____ brought water up to the tree's branches and leaves.

6. The fighter _____ backward after he was shoved.

7. The dogs heard "_____" and turned to the right.

GO TO PART D IN YOUR TEXTBOOK

A STORY DETAILS

Work the items.

1. When the boat flipped over, Thornton ▮▮▮ .

   a. drowned   b. was flung out

   c. swam to shore

2. When the boat flipped over, Buck ▮▮▮ .

   a. dove into the river

   b. barked wildly

   c. ran along the river

3. Hans and Pete attached a ▮▮▮ to Buck after his first attempt to rescue Thornton.

   a. chain   b. rope   c. lifeboat

4. Then what did Hans and Pete do with Buck?

   a. held him back

   b. had him pull them out to Thornton

   c. threw him into the river

5. After Buck and Thornton got back to shore, they ▮▮▮ .

   a. ate a hearty meal   b. passed out

   c. thanked Hans and Pete

6. Later, Thornton said that Buck could pull ▮▮▮ pounds.

   a. 100   b. 500   c. 1,000

7. How far did Thornton say Buck could pull that weight?

   a. 100 yards   b. 100 feet

   c. 100 meters

8. How much money did Matthewson offer if Buck could pull that load?

   a. 100 dollars   b. 1,000 dollars

   c. 10,000 dollars

B VOCABULARY

Complete each sentence with the correct word.

clutch	jut	slosh
flushes	lean	stretch
guilty	rears	treacherous

1. Someone who makes a mistake is

   _____ of the mistake.

2. When rocks stick out from a river, they

   _____ out of the river.

3. The water moved slowly in the flattest

   _____ of the river.

4. When you grab onto something, you

   _____ it with your hands.

5. When an animal stands on its hind legs,

   it _____ up.

6. When your face turns red and hot, it

   _____ .

7. Something that is very dangerous is

   _____ .

C | VOCABULARY REVIEW

Complete each sentence with the correct word.

coils	grapple	naked
embrace	haunt	recover
exchange	ideal	tolerate

1. The soldiers dropped their guns and began to _____ with their bare hands.

2. Anita could no longer _____ the cold weather, so she went back inside.

3. All the kids wanted to _____ the cute puppy.

4. After a week, Jammal began to _____ from the flu.

5. There were several _____ of rope on the boat's deck.

6. Warm summer days have _____ weather for a picnic.

7. You need a receipt to _____ products you buy at a store.

D | MAIN IDEA

Write a complete main-idea sentence for each paragraph.

1. Last summer, the Chavez family got on a train in Los Angeles. The train pulled out of the Los Angeles station at night and started heading east. The next morning, it passed through Denver. That night, it stopped in Chicago, but the Chavez family did not get off. After one more night, the train finally arrived in New York City. The Chavez family got off the train and walked into the train station.

_____

_____

_____

2. It was springtime, and all the people around Liverpool were talking about the steeplechase that was coming up. People talked about all the different horses, but nobody talked about Chico, a brown horse with white spots. On the day of the steeplechase, Chico lined up with all the other horses and waited for the signal to start. The signal went off, and all the horses started running. Chico was far behind at first, but as the race continued, he came closer and closer to the lead. At the last jump, Chico took the lead, and he was the first horse to cross the finish line.

_____

_____

_____

GO TO PART E IN YOUR TEXTBOOK

A STORY DETAILS

Work the items.

1. How many dogs normally pulled Matthewson's sled?

   a. two   b. ten   c. twenty

2. What objects were on the sled?

   a. sacks of flour   b. sacks of gold

   c. sand bags

3. Buck was in ▓ condition.

   a. pretty good   b. reasonable

   c. perfect

4. Buck answered Thornton's request by ▓ .

   a. barking loudly

   b. prancing up and down

   c. seizing Thornton's hand

5. In which direction did Buck go when Thornton said "Gee"?

   a. left   b. right

   c. straight ahead

6. In which direction did Buck go when Thornton said "Haw"?

   a. left   b. right

   c. straight ahead

7. What was Thornton's third command to Buck?

   a. Go straight!   b. Whoa!

   c. Mush on!

8. How far did Buck move the sled?

   a. 100 feet   b. 100 yards

   c. 100 meters

B VOCABULARY

Complete each sentence with the correct word.

clutch	guilty	stretch
flush	lunge	witness
grates	quiver	

1. When something rubs against a hard surface and makes a harsh sound, it _____ .

2. When you see an event happening, you _____ the event.

3. When a person commits a crime, that person is _____ of the crime.

4. The rapids were in just one _____ of the river.

5. Another word for *shake* is _____ .

6. When you charge forward suddenly, you _____ .

7. They could not _____ the slippery rock with their wet hands.

Write a complete main-idea sentence for each paragraph.

1. Saturday finally arrived. Janet grabbed her cell phone. Then she went outside to look for her friends. When she found everybody, she told them to stand together on her porch. She looked at the cell phone screen and told everybody to stand closer together. Finally, she said, "Smile," and pressed a button on the cell phone. The phone went "click," and some of Janet's friends made faces.

_____

_____

_____

2. William liked rowing boats. Last spring, William visited Swan Lake. He rented a rowboat for the whole day. He hopped into the boat and started to pull the oars. The boat started across the lake. William could see the boat rental place getting farther and farther away. William kept rowing. He looked at people fishing and at birds flying near the water. He had fun seeing how fast he could row. After a long time, he came to the opposite side of the lake.

_____

_____

_____

GO TO PART D IN YOUR TEXTBOOK

A RHYME SCHEME

Fill in the blanks to show the rhyme scheme. Write:

- **A** if the last word rhymes with *pain*.
- **B** if the last word rhymes with *ping* or *pings*.
- **C** if the last word rhymes with *by*.
- **D** if the last word rhymes with *day*.
- **E** if the last word rhymes with *furls*.
- **F** if the last word rhymes with *do*.
- **G** if the last word rhymes with *wife*.

In time of silver rain _____

The butterflies lift silken wings _____

To catch a rainbow cry, _____

And trees put forth new leaves to

sing _____

In joy beneath the sky _____

As down the roadway _____

Passing boys and girls _____

Go singing, too, _____

In time of silver rain _____

When spring _____

And life _____

Are new. _____

B VOCABULARY

Complete each sentence with the correct word.

beam	drowsy	quiver
bough	lullaby	stanza
couplet	lunge	witness

1. A group of lines in a poem is called a

   _____.

2. A pair of lines that rhyme in a poem is

   called a _____.

3. A main branch of a tree is called a

   _____.

4. The boy was so scared that he began to

   _____.

5. Few people are able to

   _____ a tiger in the wild.

6. A ray of light is sometimes called a

   _____ of light.

7. A song that is used to put children to sleep

   is called a _____ .

C RHYME SCHEME

Fill in the blanks to show the rhyme scheme. Write:

- **A** if the last word rhymes with *run*.
- **B** if the last word rhymes with *might*.
- **C** if the last word rhymes with *my*.
- **D** if the last word rhymes with *go*.

They are the first when day's begun ____

To touch the beams of morning sun, ____

They are the last to hold the light ____

When evening changes into night. ____

And when a moon floats on the sky, ____

They hum a drowsy lullaby ____

Of sleepy children long ago ... ____

Trees are the kindest things I know. ____

D VOCABULARY REVIEW

Complete each sentence with the correct word.

embraced	haunt	rear
grapple	ideal	recover
grate	jut	tolerate

1. Yoshi needed several weeks to

   _____ from his
   knee operation.

2. A kayak is the _____ boat
   for going down rapids.

3. The crowd watched the wrestlers

   _____ on the mat.

4. The goat had to _____ up
   to reach the leaves in the tree.

5. The teacher was nice, but he would not

   _____ bad behavior.

6. You should lift chairs when you
   carry them so their legs don't

   _____ against the floor.

7. The mother _____ her child
   every morning.

GO TO PART E IN YOUR TEXTBOOK

A STORY DETAILS

Work the items.

1. On which continent do scarlet tanagers spend the summer?

   _____

2. On which continent do they spend the winter?

   _____

3. When tanagers shed their old feathers and grow new ones, they are [ ] .

   a. molding   b. molting

   c. mulching

4. When tanagers migrate, they fly [ ] .

   a. during the day

   b. during the night

   c. all the time

5. Tanagers spend the winter in a place that is [ ] .

   a. rainy   b. cold   c. dry

6. To identify the rivers salmon were born in, scientists [ ] their fins in different locations.

   a. tied ribbons to   b. tagged

   c. clipped

7. The [ ] is the largest salmon.

   a. chinook   b. coho   c. pink

8. During a salmon run, the salmon swim [ ] .

   a. downstream   b. upstream

   c. in the ocean

9. Places where salmon lay their eggs are called [ ] grounds.

   a. nesting   b. trawling

   c. spawning

B VOCABULARY

Complete each sentence with the correct word.

beam	identify	plentiful
bough	lullaby	spawn
drowsy	migrate	volunteer

1. Whenever help was needed, the girl was happy to _____ .

2. When salmon return to their home rivers, they lay their _____ .

3. The travelers used labels to _____ their suitcases.

4. Scarlet tanagers _____ from North America to South America every year.

5. Apples were _____ in the beautiful orchard.

6. Fletcher felt so _____ that he decided to stay in bed.

7. Juanita held onto a strong _____ when she began climbing the tree.

C POETRY WORDS

Work the items.

1. The groups of lines in poems are called ▢ .

   a. beats   b. meters   c. stanzas

2. The pattern of strong and weak syllables in a poem is called the ▢ .

   a. stanza   b. meter   c. rhythm

3. Strong syllables in a poem are called ▢ .

   a. beats   b. rhythm   c. stanzas

4. The meter in a poem is the number of ▢ per line.

   a. beats   b. rhythms   c. stanzas

5. Poems that have strong rhythm and meter are called ▢

   a. stanzas   b. verse   c. couplets

6. A pair of lines that rhyme is called a rhyming ▢ .

   a. couplet   b. meter   c. beat

D STRUCTURAL ELEMENTS OF POETRY

Write S below each strong syllable and w below each weak syllable.

1. They   do   no   harm,   they   sim-   ply   grow
   ___   ___   ___   ___   ___   ___   ___   ___

2. And   spread   a   shade   for   slee-   py   cows.
   ___   ___   ___   ___   ___   ___   ___   ___

3. The   mouse   ran   up   the   clock.
   ___   ___   ___   ___   ___   ___

4. Dou-   ble,   dou-   ble,   toil   and   trou-   ble
   ___   ___   ___   ___   ___   ___   ___   ___

5. And   all   that   migh-   ty   heart   is   ly-   ing   still
   ___   ___   ___   ___   ___   ___   ___   ___   ___   ___

6. Hi-   ckor-   y,   di-   ckor-   y   dock
   ___   ___   ___   ___   ___   ___   ___

7. In   the   blink   of   an   eye
   ___   ___   ___   ___   ___   ___

GO TO PART D IN YOUR TEXTBOOK

A STORY DETAILS

Work the items.

1. Woodchucks are closely related to ▨ .

   a. bears   b. woodpeckers

   c. squirrels

2. Woodchucks eat ▨ .

   a. wood   b. meat   c. vegetables

3. During winter, woodchucks ▨ .

   a. migrate   b. hibernate

   c. look for food

4. During winter, the woodchuck's heart beats ▨ times a minute.

   a. 4   b. 40   c. 80

5. The animal that hatches from a butterfly's eggs begins as a ▨ .

   a. worm   b. caterpillar

   c. butterfly

6. Butterflies form inside cases called ▨ .

   a. macaroons   b. monsoons

   c. cocoons

7. What sweet liquid do butterflies drink?

   _____

8. In which country are the Sierra Madre mountains located?

   _____

9. Some trees in those mountains turn orange during the winter because they are covered with ▨ .

   a. mold   b. caterpillars

   c. butterflies

B VOCABULARY

Complete each sentence with the correct word.

commotion	identify	plentiful
deflate	migrate	spawn
enlarge	mysterious	volunteer

1. Something that is full of mystery is

   _____ .

2. A noisy disturbance is called a

   _____ .

3. When something is in good supply, it is

   _____ .

4. Fish eggs are called _____ .

5. When you make something larger, you

   _____ it.

6. When you let air out of a tire, you

   _____ the tire.

7. When you move from one area to another

   area, you _____ to the other area.

C POETRY WORDS

Complete each sentence with the correct word.

beats	rhythm
couplet	stanza
meter	verse

1. The line "Hickory dickory dock" has three
   _____ .

2. Poems with strong rhythm and meter are
   called _____ .

3. The _____ for the line
   "It came upon a midnight clear" is a weak
   syllable followed by a strong syllable.

4. The _____ for the line
   "I wandered, lonely as a cloud" is four beats.

5. The following lines are an example of a
   rhyming _____ :
   Jack be nimble, Jack be quick
   Jack jump over the candlestick

D STRUCTURAL ELEMENTS OF POETRY

Write S below each strong syllable and w below each weak syllable.

1. Not   a   crea-   ture   was   stir-   ring,   not   e-   ven   a   mouse.
   ___   ___   ___   ___   ___   ___   ___   ___   ___   ___   ___   ___

2. The   grizz-   ly   bear   is   huge   and   wild.
   ___   ___   ___   ___   ___   ___   ___   ___

3. The   on-   ly   news   I   know
   ___   ___   ___   ___   ___   ___

4. Out   of   the   cra-   dle,   end-   less-   ly   rock-   ing
   ___   ___   ___   ___   ___   ___   ___   ___   ___   ___

5. But,   soft!   what   light   through   yon-   der   win-   dow   breaks?
   ___   ___   ___   ___   ___   ___   ___   ___   ___   ___

6. A   green   and   yel-   low   bas-   ket
   ___   ___   ___   ___   ___   ___   ___

7. Lon-   don   bridge   is   fal-   ling   down.
   ___   ___   ___   ___   ___   ___   ___

GO TO PART D IN YOUR TEXTBOOK

A STORY DETAILS

Work the items.

1. A dog's best search tool is its ▮▮▮ .

   a. agility   b. nose   c. obedience

2. Search dogs begin their training when they are three to ten ▮▮▮ old.

   a. days   b. weeks   c. months

3. When a search dog finds something, it ▮▮▮ .

   a. keeps on going   b. gives a signal

   c. returns to its handler

4. Early training exercises for search dogs are like games of ▮▮▮ .

   a. hide-and-seek   b. tag

   c. follow the leader

5. What can send a search dog off track when it is following a scent?

   a. strong winds   b. warm weather

   c. humid air

6. Volunteers pretend to be ▮▮▮ victims by hiding in tunnels beneath the snow.

   a. flood   b. hurricane

   c. avalanche

7. Search dogs follow commands, so they are ▮▮▮ .

   a. agile   b. obedient

   c. confused

8. A dog's combination of quickness, balance, and flexibility is called ▮▮▮ .

   a. ability   b. agility   c. senility

9. Dogs can serve in real disasters if they pass the ▮▮▮ test.

   a. FEMA   b. FAME   c. FEAM

B VOCABULARY

Complete each sentence with the correct word.

agility	deflate	obedience
avalanche	enlarge	relationship
commotion	mysterious	unstable

1. The ladder was so _____ that no dogs would climb it.

2. The warm weather started a deadly _____ of snow and ice in the mountains.

3. The goat had great _____ and easily climbed the steep, rocky mountain.

4. Soldiers have to show _____ to their commanders.

5. A search and rescue dog has to have a good _____ with its handler.

6. It took a long time to _____ the gigantic balloon.

7. Woodchucks _____ rooms in their den during the spring.

C | REASONS AND EVIDENCE

Circle the sentence that makes a claim about the signals that dogs give. Then underline the sentences that give evidence to support that claim.

The relationship between dog and handler goes both ways. Handlers learn to trust their dog's instincts. A handler watches the dog closely as it searches. Search and rescue dogs may give different signals when they find something. One dog might stop moving and stand with its tail still, but another might jump into the air. Many dogs signal by barking a certain way. A handler has to know the dog's signals.

D | STRUCTURAL ELEMENTS OF POETRY

Write S below each strong syllable and w below each weak syllable.

1. Is   hung   with   bloom   a-   long   the   bough
___   ___   ___   ___   ___   ___   ___   ___

2. Catch   a   ti-   ger   by   the   toe.
___   ___   ___   ___   ___   ___   ___

3. Here   we   go   round   the   mul-   ber-   ry   bush
___   ___   ___   ___   ___   ___   ___   ___   ___

4. Old   Mc-   Do-   nald   had   a   farm
___   ___   ___   ___   ___   ___   ___

5. If   mu-   sic   be   the   food   of   love,   play   on
___   ___   ___   ___   ___   ___   ___   ___   ___   ___

6. To   catch   a   rain-   bow   cry
___   ___   ___   ___   ___   ___

GO TO PART D IN YOUR TEXTBOOK

A STORY DETAILS

Work the items.

1. Martha was the ▓▓▓ puppy in the litter.

   a. largest   b. fastest

   c. smallest

2. What did Mr. Owl want to do with Martha at first?

   a. Give her away.

   b. Train her to be a hunting dog.

   c. Keep her as a pet.

3. Mr. Owl called Martha a ▓▓▓ .

   a. hound   b. puppy   c. runt

4. Julie used a little ▓▓▓ to feed Martha.

   a. spoon   b. bottle   c. bowl

5. Martha had an unusually keen sense of ▓▓▓ .

   a. hearing   b. smell   c. taste

6. To test the puppies, Mr. Owl put a ▓▓▓ over the top of a box filled with puppies.

   a. screen   b. board

   c. piece of glass

7. Then he put ▓▓▓ just outside the box.

   a. a piece of meat   b. Martha

   c. the dogs' mother

8. The best hunting dogs were probably the ones that kept ▓▓▓ .

   a. sniffing the air

   b. banging their heads

   c. whining

B VOCABULARY

Complete each sentence with the correct word.

agility	litter	sensitive
intense	misery	tussle
limp	reluctant	

1. When you have trouble walking, you _____ .

2. A dog who can detect very faint smells has a _____ nose.

3. When you really don't want to do something, you are _____ to do it.

4. When you feel great unhappiness, you feel _____ .

5. They backed away from the fire because the heat was so _____ .

6. Puppies like to fight and _____ with each other.

7. A group of animals born to the same mother at the same time is called a _____ .

C VOCABULARY REVIEW

Complete each sentence with the correct word.

> avalanche   enlarge   relationship
> commotion   mysterious   unstable
> deflate   obedience

1. The people were puzzled by the

   _____ noise.

2. The company was growing and had to

   _____ its factory.

3. The army depended on the

   _____ of its soldiers.

4. The ladder was so _____
   that no one would climb it.

5. Geese make a loud _____
   when they see a fox.

6. Everyone on the team had a good

   _____ with the other
   players.

7. The _____ roared down the
   mountain and crashed into the ski resort.

D POETRY REVIEW

Work the items.

So   long   as   men   can   breathe   or   eyes   can   see,
___   ___   ___   ___   ___   ___   ___   ___   ___   ___

So   long   lives   this,   and   this   gives   life   to   thee.
___   ___   ___   ___   ___   ___   ___   ___   ___   ___

1. These two lines are an example of

   a rhyming _____ .

2. Write *S* under the strong syllables and *w*
   under the weak syllables.

3. The ▓▓▓ for each line is a weak syllable
   followed by strong syllable.

   a. meter   b. rhythm   c. rhyme

4. How many beats are in each line?

   _____

5. The number of beats in each line is called
   the ▓▓▓ .

   a. meter   b. rhythm   c. rhyme

6. What does *thee* mean in the second line?

   a. me   b. him   c. you

GO TO PART E IN YOUR TEXTBOOK

A STORY DETAILS

Work the items.

1. A group of puppies born to the same mother at the same time is called a ▨ .

   a. litter   b. clutch   c. kennel

2. What was the name of Mr. Owl's best hunting dog?

   _____

3. None of Mr. Owl's dogs had ever tracked an animal over the ▨ .

   a. long grass   b. path up the hill

   c. rocky ridge

4. This chapter took place during the ▨ .

   a. late fall   b. early winter

   c. late winter

5. Two of the young dogs chased a

   _____ down the other side of the rocky ridge.

6. Why didn't Mr. Owl walk home?

   a. He was too tired.

   b. He broke his leg.

   c. He got lost.

7. Julie played a game by hiding a

   _____ from Martha.

8. Martha found that object quickly because she ▨ .

   a. saw where Julie hid it   b. smelled it

   c. heard it moving

9. Mr. _____ was missing at the end of the chapter.

B VOCABULARY

Complete each sentence with the correct word.

dwarf	migrate	ridge
kennel	plentiful	spawn
ledge	quail	volunteer

1. The hungry birds flew to a place that had _____ food.

2. A flat shelf on the side of a cliff or wall is called a _____ .

3. A long, narrow hilltop is called a

   _____ .

4. During the fall, ducks _____ to warmer areas.

5. A California _____ is a bird with a crest of feathers above its head.

6. A place where dogs or cats are kept is called a _____ .

7. Another word for *very short* is

   _____ .

C REFERRING TO TEXT

Underline the sentence that explains why training a young hound to hunt takes a long time.

Even though a hound has a magnificent nose, training a young hound to hunt properly takes a long time. The problem is that a young hound wants to hunt everything. The hound may start out following the scent of a deer. But if it comes across the scent of a rabbit or a quail, the hound will quickly forget about the deer and follow the new scent. Young hounds must work hour after hour learning to stay with one scent and ignore the others.

D VOCABULARY REVIEW

Complete each sentence with the correct word.

intense	misery	sensitive
limp	relationship	tussle
litter	reluctant	unstable

1. The scared child was _____ to enter the haunted house at the fair.

2. Her fingers were so _____ that they could feel a single grain of sand.

3. Our cat came from a _____ of five kittens.

4. A cowgirl needs to have a good _____ with her horse.

5. The toddlers began to _____ in the sandbox.

6. A day of rain is a day of _____ for a child who wants to play outside.

7. The cook cried because of the _____ odor of the onions.

GO TO PART D IN YOUR TEXTBOOK

A STORY DETAILS

Work the items.

1. Why couldn't Julie's mother contact the Whitebirds?

   a. They weren't at home.

   b. The wind had blown down the phone lines.

   c. Her cell phone battery was dead.

2. Why did Julie's mother leave the house?

   a. To go for help.

   b. To search for Mr. Owl by herself.

   c. To put the dogs in the kennel.

3. Before Julie and Martha went outside, Julie held Mr. Owl's _____ in front of Martha's nose.

4. Why did Julie do that?

   a. So Martha would know what they looked like.

   b. So Martha could find more of them.

   c. So Martha could pick up Mr. Owl's scent.

5. The first animal that Martha tracked in the meadow was a _____ .

6. Julie could tell that Martha had picked up that type of scent because Martha was ▮▮▮ .

   a. barking loudly

   b. running in a circle

   c. running straight

7. When Martha caught the scent of an animal, she let out a ▮▮▮ .

   a. whine   b. long howl

   c. short bark

8. When Martha caught the scent of Mr. Owl, she let out a ▮▮▮ .

   a. whine   b. long howl

   c. short bark

B PICTURE CLUES

Work the items.

  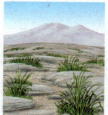

   A   B   C

1. Which picture shows a place that would hold an animal's scent well?

   • A   • B   • C

2. Which picture shows a place that would hold a scent, but not too well?

   • A   • B   • C

3. Which picture shows a place that would hold a scent poorly?

   • A   • B   • C

4. That place would hold a scent poorly because it's ▮▮▮ .

   a. grassy   b. rocky   c. flat

C VOCABULARY

Complete each sentence with the correct word.

chime	kennel	quail
down	ledge	ridge
dwarf	old-fashioned	stocking

1. A warm coat filled with soft feathers is called a _____ coat.

2. When clocks make a ringing sound, they _____ .

3. Even a baby was taller than the _____ tree.

4. His grandmother had an _____ radio that she got when she was a child.

5. When people left town, the vet kept their dogs in a _____ .

6. A narrow _____ ran along the top of the hill.

7. Frank used knitting needles to make a _____ cap.

D TEXT STRUCTURE

Write whether each passage uses _sequence of events, comparison, cause and effect,_ or _problem and solution._

1. Alma was standing in the cold, so she started shivering.

   _____

2. Alma was standing in the cold, so she went back inside.

   _____

3. The man cut himself, so he put on a bandage.

   _____

4. Samir toasted two pieces of bread. Then he spread peanut butter on one piece and jam on the other piece. He put the two pieces of bread together and ate them for lunch.

   _____

5. Rance forgot to put gas in his car. He ran out of gas while driving.

   _____

6. The sidewalk near the school is smooth and clean, but the sidewalk near my house is cracked and full of holes.

   _____

7. Even though Rento was short, his sister was tall.

   _____

GO TO PART E IN YOUR TEXTBOOK

A STORY DETAILS

Work the items.

1. Julie had a dismal feeling about the rocky ridge because ▮ .

   a. dogs could not track there

   b. it was full of wild animals

   c. it was far away

2. Why did Julie's flashlight work only some of the time?

   a. The batteries were dead.

   b. The bulb had burned out.

   c. She damaged it when she fell.

3. What did Julie have to do to make the flashlight work?

   a. change the batteries

   b. bang it against her palm

   c. screw the bulb back in

4. Julie finally caught up to Martha at the rocky _____ .

5. Julie noticed two dots of _____ in the valley to the south.

6. Julie used her _____ to signal to the people in the valley.

7. Which person did **not** approach Julie on the ridge?

   a. Mr. Whitebird   b. Mr. Taylor

   c. Mr. Owl

8. At the end of the chapter, Martha caught scent of a _____ .

B VOCABULARY

Complete each sentence with the correct word.

cast	face	old-fashioned
chimed	goose	sprawled
down	hoarse	unexpectedly

1. Trying to find a needle in a haystack is like a wild _____ chase.

2. Saleem fell off his bicycle and _____ across the pavement.

3. No matter how much it _____ , the hound couldn't find the scent.

4. The mountain climbers moved slowly up the _____ of the cliff.

5. His watch _____ once an hour.

6. The fire alarm went off _____ , so the students got ready to leave the classroom.

7. Rashida yelled so loudly at the soccer game that she became _____ .

C TEXT STRUCTURE

Work the items.

1. When tanagers arrive in May to spend the late spring and summer in North America, they are in what scientists call summer dress. The wing and tail feathers of the male birds are jet black, and the rest of their feathers are bright red. The female birds' feathers are greenish-yellow.

- Which text structure does paragraph 1 use?

  a. sequence of events

  b. comparison

  c. cause and effect

  d. problem and solution

2. During September, the days grow shorter. The weather gets colder, and the insects that tanagers eat become scarce. So the birds begin moving southward.

- Which text structure does paragraph 2 use?

  a. sequence of events

  b. comparison

  c. cause and effect

  d. problem and solution

3. Tanagers fly during the night. Each morning, the birds land and eat as many insects, fruits, and seeds as they can. Then they rest and eat some more. At dusk, their long journey continues.

- Which text structure does paragraph 3 use?

  a. sequence of events

  b. comparison

  c. cause and effect

  d. problem and solution

D PICTURE CLUES

Work the items.

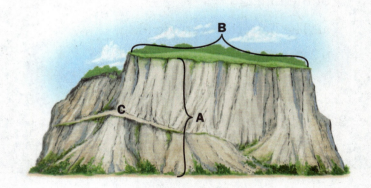

1. Which letter shows the face? _____

2. Which letter shows the ridge? _____

3. Which letter shows the ledge? _____

GO TO PART D IN YOUR TEXTBOOK

A STORY DETAILS

Work the items.

1. When Martha was tracking Mr. Owl's scent, she ▮▮▮ .

   a. howled   b. barked

   c. whined

2. Julie gave her father's scent to Martha by letting her smell his _____ .

3. Which dog did **not** stay with Mr. Owl?

   a. Leader   b. Boomer

   c. Yodeler

4. Julie and the other people knew they had found Mr. Owl when they ▮▮▮ him.

   a. saw   b. heard   c. smelled

5. The men fastened some _____ around Mr. Owl's leg.

6. Mr. Owl was talking to ▮▮▮ when he said, "Nobody's going to give you away."

   a. Martha's smallest puppy

   b. Martha's largest puppy

   c. Martha

7. Julie's operation was successful in one way because it helped her walk ▮▮▮ .

   a. perfectly   b. longer

   c. better

8. Julie's operation was unsuccessful in one way because she still had a ▮▮▮ .

   a. limp   b. cast   c. broken leg

B VOCABULARY

Complete each sentence with the correct word.

abandon	face	intently
acre	flyer	operate
cast	hoarse	sprawl

1. A piece of paper with an ad on it is called a _____ .

2. When you do something _____ , you concentrate on that thing.

3. When doctors _____ , they cut into someone's body.

4. It was hard to climb the _____ of the cliff.

5. When you leave a place without planning to come back, you _____ that place.

6. Her voice was _____ from so much yelling.

7. The dog began to _____ for the deer's scent.

C CHARACTER STATEMENTS

Complete each sentence with *beginning* or *end*.

1. At the _____ of the story, Julie's father might have said, "We don't want any runts in our kennel."

2. At the _____ of the story, Julie might have said, "Martha is the best hunting dog in North Carolina."

3. At the _____ of the story, Julie's father might have said, "I'll never give a runt away again."

4. At the _____ of the story, Julie's father might have said, "Runts can grow up to be good hunters."

5. At the _____ of the story, Julie might have said, "Martha may never grow up to be a good hunting dog, but I love her."

D TEXT STRUCTURE

Work the items.

1. A dog's best search tool is its nose. A dog's sense of smell can be one thousand to ten thousand times stronger than a human's sense of smell.

• Which text structure does paragraph 1 use?

  a. sequence of events

  b. comparison

  c. cause and effect

  d. problem and solution

2. Early training exercises are like games of hide-and-seek. At first the game is simple. A search and rescue dog may watch its handler go into a nearby area and hide. The handler then gives a command for the dog to find the handler. Gradually the game gets harder.

• Which text structure does paragraph 2 use?

  a. sequence of events

  b. comparison

  c. cause and effect

  d. problem and solution

3. There is often a lot of commotion at a rescue site, and the search and rescue dog must ignore the racket and focus on its work. The only signals the dog attends to are voice signals and hand signals from the handler.

• Which text structure does paragraph 3 use?

  a. sequence of events

  b. comparison

  c. cause and effect

  d. problem and solution

GO TO PART D IN YOUR TEXTBOOK

A STORY DETAILS

Work the items.

1. Which state was in the middle of the Dust Bowl?

   a. Kansas   b. Texas

   c. Oklahoma

2. What did farmers in that state have to plow before they could plant wheat?

   a. sod   b. rocks

   c. swamps

3. What happened to wheat prices during World War One?

   a. They stayed the same.

   b. They went down.

   c. They went up.

4. What happened to wheat prices after World War One?

   a. They stayed the same.

   b. They went down.

   c. They went up.

5. What type of weather pattern began in the Dust Bowl in 1931?

   a. heat wave   b. drought

   c. cold spell

6. What loosened the soil and created dust?

   a. rain   b. heat   c. plowing

7. What spread dust around the Dust Bowl?

   a. wind   b. floods

   c. earthquakes

8. People who breathed the dust developed dust ▨ .

   a. ammonia   b. nemesis

   c. pneumonia

9. Another name for California was the ▨ State.

   a. Paradise   b. Golden   c. Garden

B VOCABULARY

Complete each sentence with the correct word.

drought	laborer	produced
eliminate	paradise	sod
extensive	pneumonia	unexpectedly

1. The best way to _____ weeds is to pull them out by the roots.

2. During a _____ , very little rain falls.

3. They hired a _____ to dig the ditch.

4. The flood was so _____ that it covered the entire city.

5. When you have _____ , you cough a lot.

6. Farmers in Oklahoma had to plow the _____ before they could plant crops.

7. Farms in the Dust Bowl _____ very little wheat during the 1930s.

C MAPS

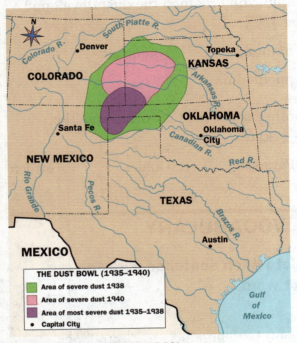

The Dust Bowl (1935–1940)

Work the items.

1. Which area had the most severe dust during the Dust Bowl?

   a. green   b. pink   c. purple

2. Which area had severe dust in 1938?

   a. green   b. pink   c. purple

3. Which river runs on the border between Oklahoma and Texas?

   a. Canadian   b. Red   c. Brazos

4. In which state is Topeka located?

   a. Kansas   b. Colorado

   c. New Mexico

5. Which state has a city that's named after the state?

   a. Colorado   b. Texas

   c. Oklahoma

D TEXT STRUCTURE

Write whether each paragraph uses *cause and effect*, *comparison*, *problem and solution*, or *sequence of events*.

1. Oklahoma was in the middle of the Dust Bowl. Farm families had begun moving to the state in the late 1800s. They had plowed millions of acres of tough sod and then planted wheat. The grain grew well in the flat, sprawling fields—as long as rain fell.

   • Which text structure does paragraph 1 use?

   _____

2. The demand for wheat increased in 1914. European countries were fighting World War One, and farmers in those countries were not able to produce as many crops. This meant more good news for farmers in America. The price of American wheat increased as supplies in Europe dropped.

   • Which text structure does paragraph 2 use?

   _____

3. The wind blasted topsoil into powdery dust, sometimes piling it into dunes. Plants were eliminated from the landscape. With nothing to graze, many animals starved. Others died from breathing or swallowing too much dust. Countless people suffered from "dust pneumonia," which caused them to cough up mud. People of all ages lost their lives to this disease.

   • Which text structure does paragraph 3 use?

   _____

GO TO PART E IN YOUR TEXTBOOK

A STORY DETAILS

Work the items.

1. The migrants who left the Dust Bowl were called _____ .

2. The migrants traveled in beat-up old cars or trucks called _____ .

3. Growers in California wanted to ▆▆▆ the supply of labor.

   a. decrease   b. increase

   c. not change

4. Growers wanted to do that so they could ▆▆▆ .

   a. lower wages   b. raise wages

   c. decrease demand

5. Why did local residents resent the migrants?

   a. The migrants bought up all the houses.

   b. The migrants drove down their wages.

   c. The migrants had the best cars.

6. During the 1930s, migrants in California earned ▆▆▆ per hour for picking lettuce and potatoes.

   a. twenty cents   b. two dollars

   c. twenty dollars

7. Who built farm labor camps for the migrants?

   a. the growers

   b. the state government

   c. the federal government

8. How many rooms did each cabin have in the farm labor camps?

   a. one   b. two   c. three

9. Who built Weedpatch School?

   a. a local building company

   b. the federal government

   c. the students and teachers

B VOCABULARY

Complete each sentence with the correct word.

determined	laborer	poverty
drought	misled	produce
extensive	paradise	resent

1. Dafna began to _____ her classmates because they made fun of her.

2. The team was _____ to win the game.

3. People were _____ by the false advertising.

4. Domingo's family lived in _____ , so he never had any money.

5. The huge farm's _____ fields stretched in every direction.

6. Mr. Han hired a _____ to help dig the ditch.

7. The flyers claimed that California was a _____ , but it wasn't.

C TEXT STRUCTURE

Write whether each paragraph uses *cause and effect, comparison, problem and solution,* **or** *sequence of events.*

1. When the jalopies broke down, the Okies would try to find odd jobs in nearby towns. The money they earned would pay for repairs, gas, or oil. While the families were waiting for repairs, they camped in or near their car or truck. At night they lit a campfire. If they were lucky, they cooked a bit of food.

- Which text structure does paragraph 1 use?

_____

2. As the supply of labor increased, the wages workers received dropped. Local residents resented the Okies who had come in and driven down their wages. When a job opened, three or four workers fought to get it. If one person refused to work for only 25 cents an hour, plenty of others would agree to such low wages. No family could live on so little income, but for many the income was better than nothing.

- Which text structure does paragraph 2 use?

_____

3. Hart won the election. One of his top goals was to help migrant children fit in at the public schools they attended. But he found that it was too difficult for them to fit in. Hart decided that the only way migrant children could receive the education they deserved was for them to

have their own school. He rented 10 acres of land next to Weedpatch Camp and hired really good teachers.

- Which text structure does paragraph 3 use?

_____

D VOCABULARY REVIEW

Complete each sentence with the correct word.

abandon	flyer	operate
acre	goose	pneumonia
eliminate	intently	sod

1. When you have _____ , you cough and have trouble breathing.

2. The field had a thick layer of

_____ .

3. The house came with one

_____ of property.

4. Some people thought the Okies were

headed on a wild _____ chase.

5. They saw a _____ about a concert on the bulletin board.

6. The cat stared _____ at the mouse hole.

7. It takes a lot of work to

_____ all the weeds from a lawn.

GO TO PART D IN YOUR TEXTBOOK

A STORY DETAILS

Work the items.

1. "The Circuit" takes place during the ▨ .

   a. 1930s   b. 1940s   c. 1950s

2. "The Circuit" takes place in the state of ▨ .

   a. Oklahoma   b. California

   c. Jalisco

3. *Ya es hora* means ▨ .

   a. that's everything   b. my old pot

   c. it's time

4. The narrator's family moved from the strawberry farm to _____ .

5. *Carcanchita* means ▨ .

   a. jalopy   b. can opener

   c. farmworker from Mexico

6. Papa thought the man who used to own his car was important because the man left a blue _____ behind the rear seat.

7. Mama's old large pot was ▨ .

   a. as big as a gallon

   b. in perfect condition

   c. galvanized

8. The walls in the garage the narrator moved into have been eaten by ▨ .

   a. earthworms   b. cockroaches

   c. termites

9. The narrator's name is

   _____ .

B VOCABULARY

Complete each sentence with the correct word.

braceros	detect	sharecropper
carcanchita	kerosene	
circuit	listo	

1. They used a _____ lamp to light the shack.

2. When he heard his mother say " _____ ," Paco knew that everything was ready.

3. The workers picking apples from the trees included several _____ from Mexico.

4. Isabel spent all summer fixing the _____ until it was ready to drive.

5. Dogs are able to _____ smells that people can't.

6. The bicycle race made a _____ around the town.

C | POETRY REVIEW

Work the items.

She walks in beauty, like the night
Of cloudless climes and starry skies;
And all that's best of dark and bright
Meet in her aspect and her eyes.

1. The rhyme scheme for these lines is ▮▮▮ .

   a. AABB   b. ABAB   c. ABCD

2. How many strong syllables are in each line?

   _____

3. So how many beats are in each line?

   _____

4. The number of beats in each line is called
   the ▮▮▮ .

   a. meter   b. rhythm   c. rhyme

5. The pattern for each line in the poem is a
   ▮▮▮ syllable followed by ▮▮▮ syllable.

   a. strong / weak   b. weak / strong

   c. strong / strong

6. In the second line, the word *climes*
   means ▮▮▮ .

   a. climbs   b. clouds   c. climates

7. In the fourth line, the word *aspect*
   means ▮▮▮ .

   a. face   b. feet   c. darkness

D | VOCABULARY REVIEW

**Complete each sentence with the
correct word.**

abandon	eliminate	operate
acre	flyer	pneumonia
determined	misled	sod

1. The family tried to _____
   the ants in their kitchen by using
   bug spray.

2. Other runners dropped out, but Imena was
   _____ to finish the race.

3. The sharecropper rented just one
   _____ from the farmer.

4. Mrs. Compton designed a
   _____ to promote her new
   pet store.

5. The criminal _____ the
   police by telling lies.

6. Hondo thought he had
   _____ , but his doctor said
   it was just the flu.

7. When the wildfire came closer, the Garcias
   had to _____ their home.

GO TO PART E IN YOUR TEXTBOOK

A STORY DETAILS

Work the items.

1. The temperature in the vineyard was almost _____ degrees when Panchito got sick.

2. Panchito got sick because he drank too much _____ .

3. Papa turned pale when he saw a ▮ .
   a. mountain lion   b. rattlesnake
   c. school bus

4. Papa said, "Tienen que tener ▮ ."
   a. cuidado   b. vámonos
   c. carcanchita

5. Papa, Roberto, and Panchito earned _____ dollars altogether on their first day working in the vineyard.

6. Panchito was able to ▮ after grape season was over.
   a. keep working   b. go to school
   c. make more money

7. The sixth-grade teacher was named Mr. _____ .

8. Panchito got nervous and scared when the teacher asked him to ▮ .
   a. multiply   b. read   c. write

9. The teacher said he would teach Panchito how to play the _____ .

B VOCABULARY

Complete each sentence with the correct word.

braceros	corridos	listo
carcanchita	detect	quince
circuit	kerosene	sharecropper

1. They could hear _____ playing softly on the radio.

2. Vanesa was counting in fives in Spanish, so she said, "Cinco (5), diez (10), _____ (15), veinte (20)."

3. The campers' flashlight batteries went dead, so they had to use _____ lamps instead.

4. Marta had a new car, but she still loved to drive her old _____ .

5. Doctors learn how to _____ different sounds in a person's heart.

6. Someone who rents land from a farmer is called a _____ .

7. The plane made a wide _____ around the airport.

C · POINT OF VIEW

Write whether each story or poem uses *first person* or *third person* point of view.

1. "The Circuit"
   _____

2. "Adventure on the Rocky Ridge"
   _____

3. "In Time of Silver Rain"
   _____

4. "For the Love of a Man"
   _____

5. "The Cat that Walked by Himself"
   _____

6. "Trees"
   _____

7. "A Horse to Remember"
   _____

D · TEXT STRUCTURE

Write whether each paragraph uses *cause and effect, comparison, problem and solution,* or *sequence of events.*

1. The food in a natural environment keeps a wild horse's teeth in balance. All the teeth are used the same amount, so they wear down the same amount. Tame horses, on the other hand, eat food that is much less rough. Also, they do not get to eat as often.

   _____

2. Tame horses do not usually eat the gritty foods that would wear down their teeth naturally and evenly. That is why they need dentists. Horse dentists use tools to wear down and smooth the horses' teeth.

   _____

3. Tame horses do not need to work as hard to grind their food. Therefore, sharp edges and points form on the parts of the teeth that are not being used much. These sharp edges and points can be very painful for a horse.

   _____

GO TO PART E IN YOUR TEXTBOOK

A STORY DETAILS

Work the items.

1. Endangered animals are animals in danger of ▉ .

   a. domestication   b. overpopulation

   c. extinction

2. Which one of the following animals is **not** endangered?

   a. chimpanzees   b. goats

   c. rhinoceroses   d. African elephants

3. One reason people hunt certain animals is because they think those animals ▉ .

   a. deserve to be protected

   b. are pests

   c. are smarter than people

4. The Carolina _____ was overhunted to extinction.

5. Wild animals that live in an area for a long time are called ▉ animals.

   a. native   b. domesticated

   c. invasive

6. When people introduce a new species to an area, the wild animals that live in the area can become ▉ .

   a. less dangerous   b. easier to tame

   c. endangered

7. ▉ forests are home to almost half the world's plant and animal species.

   a. Arid   b. Rain   c. Dwarf

8. Which one of the following is an example of habitat destruction?

   a. people remodeling their apartments

   b. people clearing land for a house

   c. people purchasing building materials

9. A large area where tigers live is called a tiger ▉ .

   a. reserve   b. resort   c. farm

B FACT OR FICTION

Write whether each item is *fact* or *fiction*.

1. Dogs can be brave. _____

2. Dogs can speak English to people.

   _____

3. Dogs are domesticated animals.

   _____

4. People can visit the Land of Oz.

   _____

5. The Land of Oz is surrounded by a desert.

   _____

6. L. Frank Baum wrote *The Wonderful Wizard of Oz.* _____

C VOCABULARY

Complete each sentence with the correct word.

endangered	reserve	species
extinct	resources	vineyard
habitat	savor	

1. A type of plant or animal is called a

   _____ of plant or animal.

2. When a type of plant or animal no longer

   exists, that type is _____ .

3. When a type of plant or animal is in
   danger of no longer existing, that type is

   _____ .

4. A place set aside for wild animals is

   called a _____ .

5. The natural home of a plant or animal is

   called its _____ .

6. Another word for *supplies* is

   _____

7. When you enjoy something completely,

   you _____ it..

D POINT OF VIEW

Complete each sentence with *firsthand*, *secondhand*, *first-person* or *third-person*.

1. An account of an event written by
   someone who experienced the event and
   uses words like **I, me, we,** and **us** is a

   _____

   account.

2. A story told by a narrator who doesn't
   appear in the story and does **not** use
   words like **I, me, we,** and **us** has a

   _____ point

   of view.

3. A story told by a narrator who appears in
   the story and uses words like **I, me, we,**
   and **us** has a

   _____ point

   of view.

4. An account of an event written by
   someone who did not experience the event

   is a _____

   account.

5. A story that includes the sentence, "We
   live in the heart of Chicago," has a

   _____ point

   of view.

6. An account that includes the sentence,
   "The guide thought about my request to
   explore the cave a little deeper," has is

   _____

   account.

GO TO PART D IN YOUR TEXTBOOK

A STORY DETAILS

Work the items.

1. European sailors first arrived on the Galápagos Islands during the

   _____ century.

2. Why didn't the Galápagos tortoises try to escape from the sailors?

   a. They wanted to be domesticated.

   b. The sailors were kind to them.

   c. They weren't afraid of people.

3. The sailors killed the tortoises because the sailors ▢ .

   a. were afraid of the tortoises

   b. wanted to eat the tortoises.

   c. wanted to use the tortoise shells for helmets.

4. The tortoises had to compete with

   _____ for plant food.

5. The orangutan is a very ▢ animal.

   a. extinct   b. solitary

   c. common

6. Orangutans live in dense ▢ .

   a. forests   b. brush   c. grass

7. The poison that hurt peregrine falcons

   was called _____ .

8. That poison ▢ the shells of falcon eggs.

   a. thinned   b. thickened

   c. enlarged

9. Real eggs in falcon nests were replaced with plaster eggs to keep the real eggs from ▢ .

   a. growing too big

   b. being poisoned

   c. cracking

B CAUSE AND EFFECT

For each animal, show two reasons why it is or was endangered.

1. Tiger

   a. overhunting

   b. competition with foreign species

   c. habitat destruction

2. Galápagos tortoise

   a. overhunting

   b. competition with foreign species

   c. pollution

3. Orangutan

   a. overhunting

   b. competition with foreign species

   c. habitat destruction

C | VOCABULARY

Complete each sentence with the correct word.

century	endangered	solitary
confined	extinct	species
declined	habitat	

1. The man was a _____ person who lived alone in the forest.

2. When one type of animal dies out all over the world, that animal is

   _____ .

3. A type of plant is a _____ of plant.

4. When people cleared land, they destroyed the owls' _____ .

5. Cars were invented more than a

   _____ ago.

6. The prisoner was _____ to a small cell.

7. When an animal is

   _____ , it is threatened with extinction.

8. When the factory left town, the population

   _____ .

D | REASONS AND EVIDENCE

Show whether each statement *supports* or *does not support* the claim.

Claim: DDT caused the decline in falcon populations.

1. Falcons can make vertical dives at up to two hundred miles per hour.

   a. supports

   b. does not support

2. Falcon populations began to decline after DDT was first used.

   a. supports

   b. does not support

3. Falcons ate animals that ate insects with DDT.

   a. supports

   b. does not support

4. Thousands of falcons have been released into the wild since the 1980s.

   a. supports

   b. does not support

5. DDT caused falcon eggshells to thin, so the eggs did not hatch.

   a. supports

   b. does not support

GO TO PART D IN YOUR TEXTBOOK

A STORY DETAILS

Work the items.

1. The person telling this biography is a ▨ .

   a. real person   b. fictional narrator

   c. major league baseball player

2. In which city does the narrator live?

   a. Chicago   b. Los Angeles

   c. New York City

3. The first African American to play major

   league baseball was _____

   _____ .

4. In what year did he first play in the major

   leagues? _____

5. The team he played for was the

   _____

   _____ .

6. When he played his first game with that
   team, he looked like the ▨ person in the
   world.

   a. happiest   b. proudest

   c. loneliest

7. His team played in _____
   Field.

B VOCABULARY

Complete each sentence with the correct word.

biography	confine	dugout
bold	daring	major
century	decline	plant

1. The old tortoise had lived for more than a

   _____ .

2. A league with the best players is called a

   _____ league.

3. Another word for *factory* is

   _____ .

4. A history of a person's life written by
   somebody else is called a

   _____ .

5. The batters who weren't hitting watched
   the baseball game from the

   _____ .

6. A person who is confident and brave is

   _____ .

7. A person who takes risks is

   _____ .

C RELATED FACTS

Work the items.

1. When a baseball team is not batting, how many of its players are in the field?

   _____

2. The catcher plays right behind the

   _____ .

3. The _____ stands right behind the catcher.

4. After a batter hits the baseball, he or she starts running toward

   _____ base.

5. To score a run, the runner has to touch

   _____ plate.

6. The _____ stands between the second baseman and the third baseman.

D TEXT STRUCTURE

Work the item.

Little was done to help the tortoises until 1959, when the Charles Darwin Foundation was created. To help the tortoises make a comeback, the Foundation set up a breeding station on one of the islands. Tortoise eggs are brought there to hatch, and the young tortoises live in safety until they are too big to be eaten by other animals. Meanwhile, goats have been removed from the islands so that there will be enough plants for the tortoises to eat.

1. Which main text structure does the paragraph use?

   a. cause and effect

   b. comparison

   c. problems and solution

   d. sequence of events

E PICTURE CLUES

Work the items.

A   B   C

1. Picture _____ shows a place that would hold an animal's scent well.

2. Picture _____ shows a place that would hold a scent, but not too well.

3. Picture _____ shows a place that would hold a scent poorly.

GO TO PART E IN YOUR TEXTBOOK

A   STORY DETAILS

Work the items.

1. The general manager of the Dodgers was

    named _____

    _____ .

2. One of the meat-packing plant workers
   said, "When you're against one player,
   you're against ▓▓▓ ."

    a. another player   b. the whole team

    c. major league baseball

3. The narrator got on Robinson's side after
   the Dodgers played the ▓▓▓ .

    a. Yankees   b. Giants

    c. Phillies

4. What did the players on that team do to
   Robinson?

    a. beat him up   b. called him names

    c. refused to play with him

5. Robinson responded to those players by
   ▓▓▓ them.

    a. ignoring   b. fighting

    c. insulting

6. What did the Dodger shortstop do to show
   he was on Robinson's side?

    a. stormed into the other team's dugout

    b. put his arm around Robinson's shoulder

    c. ignored the other team

7. Robinson made pitchers nervous by

    _____ bases.

8. In 1947, the Dodgers won the

    _____ League pennant.

9. Also in 1947, Robinson won the ▓▓▓ of the
   Year award.

    a. Batter   b. Fielder   c. Rookie

B   PICTURE CLUES

Work the items.

	1	2	3	4	5	6	7	8	9
Phillies	0	1	2	3	0	0	2	0	0
Dodgers	0	0	1	0	1	2	0	0	1

1. The game lasted for _____
   innings.

2. The team that scored first was the

    _____ .

3. That team first scored in the

    _____ inning.

4. The Dodgers scored _____
   run in the ninth inning.

5. The team that won the game was the

    _____ .

6. The final score was Phillies

    _____ , Dodgers

    _____ .

C VOCABULARY

Complete each sentence with the correct word.

biography	insult	plant
dugout	major	rookie
inning	pennant	steal

1. The runner was out when she tried to _____ a base.

2. The player had a lot to learn during his _____ year on the team.

3. The Dodgers scored three runs in the top of the third _____ .

4. The bully tried to _____ the other students by making rude comments.

5. The Dodgers won the National League _____ in 1947.

6. Working at a steel _____ is a dangerous job.

7. Many people wanted to read the new _____ of Abraham Lincoln.

D RELATED FACTS

Work the items.

1. When a baseball team is not batting, how many of its players are in the field? _____

2. A baseball game lasts _____ innings unless there is a tie.

3. The visiting team bats during the _____ of each inning.

4. The home team bats during the _____ of each inning.

5. Each team gets to bat until it makes _____ outs.

6. To score a run, the runner must touch _____ plate.

GO TO PART E IN YOUR TEXTBOOK

A STORY DETAILS

Work the items.

1. Robinson's family moved to the state of

   _____ when he was still

   a baby.

2. When he was young, Robinson joined the

   _____

   _____ Gang.

3. Robinson joined the gang because he
   wanted to ▩ .

   a. play sports   b. belong to a group

   c. make his mother sad

4. A mechanic told Robinson that he was
   behaving like ▩ .

   a. an athlete   b. a sheep

   c. a fan

5. Jackie's brother Mack set a junior college
   record in the ▩ .

   a. long jump   b. 200-meter dash

   c. high jump

6. Which four of these sports did Robinson
   play in junior college?

   a. football   b. hockey

   c. baseball   d. track

   e. tennis   f. golf

   g. basketball

7. One day Robinson was scheduled for a
   track meet and a baseball game. He solved
   the problem by ▩ .

   a. choosing just one event

   b. participating in both events

   c. rescheduling one event

8. Which university did Robinson attend after
   he finished junior college?

   a. UCLA   b. USC   c. UCSD

9. Robinson's poorest sport at that university

   was _____ .

B RELATED FACTS

Work the items.

1. A baseball game has _____
   innings if there is not a tie.

2. When a baseball team is not batting, it has

   _____ players on the field.

3. The visiting team bats in the

   _____ of each inning.

4. The _____ stands between
   second baseman and the third baseman.

C VOCABULARY

Complete each sentence with the correct word.

inning	mechanic	punt
insult	Olympics	quarterback
long	pennant	schedule

1. You jump as far as you can in the
   _____ jump.

2. The Summer _____ are held
   every four years.

3. The Cubs won the game in the bottom of
   the ninth _____ .

4. The football team decided to
   _____ the ball.

5. The auto _____ worked in
   a garage.

6. In a football game, the
   _____ throws the ball.

7. It was hard to _____ a
   meeting that everyone could attend.

D BIOGRAPHY REVIEW

Work the items.

1. Jackie Robinson played for the
   _____ Dodgers.

2. After the 1957 season, the Dodgers moved
   to the city of _____
   _____ .

3. When Robinson got on base, he liked
   to ▮▮▮ .
   a. stay where he was
   b. talk to the pitcher
   c. steal the next base

4. Which team won the World Series in 1947?
   a. Dodgers   b. Giants
   c. Yankees

5. In 1947, Robinson won the ▮▮▮ of the
   Year award.
   a. Rookie   b. Batter   c. Pitcher

E CLASSIFICATION

**Write the main use people have for
each animal. Choose *hunting*, *food*,
or *carrying things*.**

1. Pig _____

2. Cat _____

3. Mule _____

4. Hound _____

5. Camel _____

GO TO PART E IN YOUR TEXTBOOK

A STORY DETAILS

Work the items.

1. After Mack got an Olympic medal, he could only find ▮▮ jobs.

   a. high-paying   b. regular

   c. odd

2. In 1941, the only professional baseball teams that black players could join were in the ▮▮ leagues.

   a. Negro   b. major   c. minor

3. What war did the United States enter in 1941?

   a. World War One   b. World War Two

   c. Korean War

4. In 1942, Jackie joined the U.S. ▮▮ .

   a. Army   b. Navy   c. Air Force

5. Because he was such a strong leader in the military, Jackie became a ▮▮ .

   a. private   b. captain   c. sailor

6. Jackie wanted to marry Rachel _____ .

7. The baseball team Jackie joined in 1945 was the Kansas City _____ .

8. For which minor league city and team did Branch Rickey want Jackie to play?

   _____

   _____

9. Rickey said, "I need someone who is strong enough to take insults ▮▮ ."

   a. and fight back

   b. without fighting back

   c. without feeling them

B TIMELINES

Here are some events from Jackie Robinson's life:

• Jackie leaves UCLA.

• Jackie joins the Kansas City Monarchs.

• Jackie becomes an officer.

Write the correct event after each date on the timeline.

1945 _____

_____

1942 _____

_____

1941 _____

_____

C VOCABULARY

Complete each sentence with the correct word.

career	organization	restricted
decent	punt	schedule
officer	quarterback	scout

1. The soldiers began to go backward after the _____ told them to retreat.

2. All the players knew that a baseball _____ was watching the game carefully.

3. The car company was a large _____ that employed thousands of people.

4. You need to go to medical school if you want a _____ as a doctor.

5. Before Jackie Robinson, the major leagues were _____ to white players.

6. The job was boring, but the pay was _____ .

7. On a football team, the _____ calls the plays.

D FACT AND FICTION

Write whether each item is *fact* or *fiction*.

1. A newspaper story about an election.
   _____

2. A short story about a talking horse.
   _____

3. An encyclopedia article about horses.
   _____

4. An article about how to make shoes.
   _____

5. A novel about a girl from Kansas.
   _____

GO TO PART E IN YOUR TEXTBOOK

A STORY DETAILS

Work the items.

1. Jackie and Rachel got married during ▨ .

   a. August 1945   b. February 1946

   c. spring training

2. In Florida, how many of the other players' wives sat next to Rachel in the stands?

   a. none   b. a few   c. all of them

3. The first game after spring training was held across the river from ▨ .

   a. Montreal   b. New York City

   c. Los Angeles

4. The second time Jackie was up during that game, he hit a ▨ .

   a. single   b. double   c. home run

5. When Jackie was on third base during that game, he rattled the pitcher so much that the pitcher ▨ .

   a. threw a wild pitch

   b. stepped off the mound

   c. made a balk

6. During another game, a player from the other team put a _____ cat onto the field.

7. Jackie answered that player by letting his ▨ do the talking.

   a. bat   b. glove   c. manager

8. At the end of the season, the Royals won ▨ .

   a. the World Series

   b. the league pennant

   c. second place

9. During his season with the Royals, Jackie was the top ▨ in the league.

   a. player   b. batter   c. fielder

B TIMELINES

Here are some events from Jackie Robinson's life:

- Jackie plays for the Monarchs.
- Jackie plays for the Royals.
- Jackie joins the Army.

Write the correct event after each date on the timeline.

1946 _____

_____

1945 _____

_____

1942 _____

_____

C VOCABULARY

Complete each sentence with the correct word.

balk	cousin	organization
career	decent	restricted
contract	officer	stadium

1. The baseball _____ included a major league team and several minor league teams.

2. A _____ is what happens when a pitcher pretends to throw a pitch.

3. The fans streamed into the soccer _____ .

4. The workers had to sign a _____ with their employer.

5. The drivers slowed down when they saw the police _____ .

6. Only certain people were allowed into the _____ area.

7. A child of your aunt or uncle is your _____ .

D MAPS

Look at the map and answer the questions.

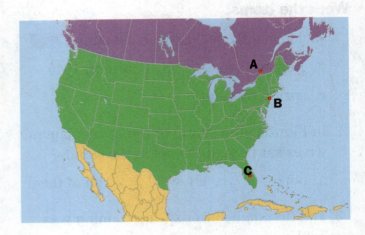

1. Which letter shows the city where Jackie Robinson played in the minor leagues? _____

2. Which letter shows the city where Jackie played in the major leagues? _____

3. Which letter shows the state where Jackie went for spring training? _____

4. In which country is Montreal located? _____

5. The country where Brooklyn is located is the _____ _____

GO TO PART D IN YOUR TEXTBOOK

A FACT GAME

Scorecard

1	2	3	4	5	6	7	8	9	10
11	12	13	14	15	16	17	18	19	20
21	22	23	24	25	26	27	28	29	30

2. Tell which character wanted each thing from Oz.

a. Courage

b. A trip back to Kansas

3. Answer the questions.

a. Which metal was discovered near Dawson in 1896?

b. Which river flows through Dawson?

4. Tell whether each thing is *fact* or *fiction*.

a. An article in an encyclopedia

b. A story about a wizard

5. Tell whether each animal is mainly used for *hunting*, *food*, or *carrying things*.

a. elephant

b. sheep

6. Tell which animal each statement describes.

a. This scarlet bird migrates to South America in the winter.

b. This fish returns to its birthplace after journeying to the ocean.

7. Tell which dog each statement describes.

a. This dog saved John Thornton's life.

b. This dog lived in Kansas.

8. Answer the questions.

a. What is the name of the horse race that includes barriers and obstacles?

b. Near which city does the Grand National Championship take place?

9. Answer the questions.

a. What's the class name for animals that do not live with people?

b. What's the class name for animals that live with people?

10. Tell which endangered animal each statement describes.

a. This large cat lives in special reserves in India.

b. This slow-moving reptile lives on the Galápagos Islands.

11. Tell which land each group of people lived in.

a. Gillikins

b. Quadlings

12. Answer the questions.

a. Who was the first African American to play major league baseball?

b. For which major league team did he play?

B STORY DETAILS

Work the items.

1. In which city did the Royals play the first three games of the 1946 Junior World Series?

   _____

2. In which city were the next three games played?

   _____

3. In which country is that city?

   _____

4. In which year did Jackie Robinson first play for the major league team in Brooklyn?

   _____

5. Which one of these National League honors did Jackie Robinson **not** win in 1949?

   a. batting championship

   b. fielding championship

   c. most valuable player

6. The two teams that played in the 1955 World Series were the Brooklyn

   _____ and the New York

   _____ .

7. The team that won the 1955 World Series

   was the _____

   _____ .

8. After which baseball season did Jackie Robinson retire from baseball?

   _____

9. One sportswriter described Jackie by writing, "He would not be ▮▮▮ . Not by the other team and not by life."

   a. annoyed   b. cheated

   c. defeated

C VOCABULARY

Complete each sentence with the correct word.

balk	defeat	honor
contract	deposit	oppose
cousin	flamingo	stadium

1. Winning an Oscar is a big

   _____ for actors.

2. Losing the basketball game by one point

   was a tough _____ for the team.

3. Before Hiro rented a trombone from the music store, she had to sign a

   _____ .

4. When robins lay eggs, they

   _____ the eggs in a nest.

5. We could tell the bird was a

   _____ because it was tall and pink.

6. You could hear fans cheering in the football

   _____ from a mile away.

7. Hannah decided to _____ Hakeen in the race for class president.

GO TO PART D IN YOUR TEXTBOOK

A STORY DETAILS

Work the items.

1. The young sea turtles in the article settle near the state of _____ .

2. The process that begins with turtle eggs hatching and ends with a turtle laying eggs is called the turtle's life ▯ .

   a. circle   b. cycle   c. cyclone

3. In which direction do rhizomes grow?

   a. horizontal   b. vertical

   c. circular

4. What grows up along a rhizome?

   a. new shoots   b. more rhizomes

   c. water

5. What part of the turtle grass plant makes it possible for turtle grass to produce seeds?

   a. roots   b. leaves   c. flowers

6. What process does turtle grass depend on to grow?

   a. photography   b. photofinishing

   c. photosynthesis

7. What is one way that sea turtles and flamingos are alike?

   a. They are both reptiles.

   b. They both lay eggs.

   c. They both have feathers.

8. What do flamingos do during the dry season?

   a. lay eggs

   b. move to a new area to find food

   c. learn to swim

9. Turtle grass and water lilies provide food and ▯ for small animals.

   a. shelter   b. water   c. warmth

B VOCABULARY

Complete each sentence with the correct word.

horizontally	polluted	typically
lumbered	rhizome	
photosynthesis	settle	

1. A _____ is a plant stem that grows in a horizontal line.

2. Plants get energy from the sun through _____ .

3. No plants or animals could live in the _____ water.

4. The family decided to _____ in a small town.

5. Rockets go into the air vertically, but cars go down the road _____ .

6. The elephants _____ across the wide plains.

C SEQUENCING

Number the events in the correct sequence. The first event has already been numbered.

__1__ A turtle lumbers up a beach until it reaches dry sand.

_____ The turtle goes back to the ocean.

_____ The turtle covers eggs with sand.

_____ The turtle digs a hole with its flippers.

_____ The turtle deposits eggs into a hole.

D TEXT STRUCTURE

Work the items.

A. The mother green sea turtle has finally lumbered all the way up the beach to the dry sand. She digs a hole in the sand with her flippers. Then she deposits more than a hundred round, white eggs into the hole. She thrashes her flippers again, covering the eggs with sand. Exhausted from her task, she drags herself back to the ocean.

1. Which main text structure does paragraph A use?

   a. cause and effect

   b. comparison

   c. problems and solution

   d. sequence of events

B. Sea grasses have roots, leaves, and flowers, just like many land plants. Sea grass flowers are small and delicate. The flowers make it possible for sea grass to produce seeds, which grow into plants the same way grass grows from seeds in a garden. So turtle grass can spread by producing seeds and by producing rhizomes.

2. Which main text structure does paragraph B use?

   a. cause and effect

   b. comparison

   c. problems and solution

   d. sequence of events

C. Not all of the coastal areas in Florida are this clean and healthy. Some areas are polluted because people have dumped garbage or oil into the water. Neither turtle grass nor turtles grow well in these polluted areas.

3. Which main text structure does paragraph B use?

   a. cause and effect

   b. comparison

   c. problems and solution

   d. sequence of events

GO TO PART E IN YOUR TEXTBOOK

A STORY DETAILS

Work the items.

1. What did Midas love most of all?

    a. his daughter   b. gold

    c. his reflection

2. What did Midas love almost as much?

    a. his daughter   b. gold

    c. his reflection

3. What kind of flowers had Midas planted in his garden?

    a. buttercups   b. roses

    c. dandelions

4. Midas used to look at those flowers and ▊ their perfume.

    a. exhale   b. reject   c. inhale

5. Midas's treasure room was in the _____ of his palace.

6. Midas spent ▊ of his time in the treasure room.

    a. all   b. a small part

    c. a large part

7. Midas felt ▊ when he was looking at his gold.

    a. happy   b. sad   c. indifferent

8. Midas was surprised to find somebody in his room because ▊ .

    a. he never had visitors

    b. there wasn't enough space for two people

    c. he had locked the door

B VOCABULARY

Complete each sentence with the correct word.

calculate	inhale	rhizome
gleam	insane	sift
horizontally	photosynthesis	

1. Rosie loved to run outside and _____ the fresh air.

2. In school, students learn how to _____ the answers to math problems.

3. On the beach, children dig up sand and let it _____ through their fingers.

4. Juan tried to make his teeth _____ by brushing them twice a day.

5. People used to think that the idea of space travel was _____ .

6. Green plants use _____ to make food.

7. A root that grows sideways is called a _____ .

C MAPS

Work the items.

1. What sea is in the middle of the map?

   a. North   b. Mediterranean

   c. Caribbean

2. What is the name of country **A**?

   _____

3. A myth from that country tells about King

   _____ .

D MYTHS

Work the items.

1. What kinds of characters often appear in myths?

   a. movie stars   b. modern children

   c. gods and goddesses

2. Many myths try to explain ▬▬ .

   a. how machines work

   b. how the world began

   c. what the world is like today

3. Some myths tell the adventures of ▬▬ .

   a. ancient heroes

   b. baseball players

   c. airplane pilots

GO TO PART E IN YOUR TEXTBOOK

A STORY DETAILS

Work the items.

1. The Golden Touch began to work at ▮▮▮ .

    a. sunrise　　b. noon　　c. sunset

2. After Midas touched the book, he couldn't ▮▮▮ it.

    a. lift　　b. open　　c. read

3. After Midas touched the book, the ▮▮▮ disappeared.

    a. pages　　b. cover

    c. wise words

4. When Midas put on his clothes, why were they heavier than usual?

    a. They were still wet.

    b. They were made of gold.

    c. Their pockets were full.

5. One soft object disturbed Midas when it changed to gold. What was that object?

    a. his pillow　　b. his handkerchief

    c. his spectacles

6. Who had made that object for Midas?

    a. the visitor　　b. his daughter

    c. his wife

7. Why couldn't Midas read anymore?

    a. His spectacles had turned to gold.

    b. He couldn't open his eyes.

    c. His books had all burned.

8. How did the roses smell before Midas touched them?

    a. They had no smell.

    b. horrible

    c. delicious

B VOCABULARY

Complete each sentence with the correct word.

appetite	envy	pity
deserves	frenzy	secure
discontented	linen	

1. Because Miguel flunked the test, he was quite _____ .

2. The sheets in the fancy hotel were made of _____ .

3. The farmer worked hard all day and had a great _____ for dinner.

4. The child ran around in a _____ , trying to clean up her room.

5. Outside it was stormy, but the family felt _____ in their well-built home.

6. Emily _____ credit for mowing the lawn.

7. All the children felt _____ for the lost puppy.

C TIMELINES

**Write the correct years in the blanks.
Choose 1941, 1947, 1955, or 1972.**

_____ Robinson leaves UCLA.

_____ Robinson dies.

_____ Robinson helps win the
World Series.

_____ Robinson first plays for
the Dodgers.

D SEQUENCING

**Number the events in the correct
sequence.**

____ Midas turned a book to gold.

____ Midas turned a rose to gold.

____ Midas asked the stranger for a favor.

____ Midas had a hard time sleeping.

E CHARACTER STATEMENTS

**Complete each sentence with _Cowardly
Lion, Cat That Walked,_ or _Ugly Duckling._**

1. "I am the king of beasts," said the

_____ .

2. "I live with people, but they can't tell me
what to do," said the

_____ .

3. "I used to be afraid of everything," said the

_____ .

4. "I finally saw who I really was when I
looked into the water," said the

_____ .

5. "I saw how the woman fooled all the other
animals," said the

_____ .

GO TO PART E IN YOUR TEXTBOOK

Name _____

A STORY DETAILS

Work the items.

1. Why did Marygold's crying surprise Midas?

   a. She was often unhappy.

   b. She was almost always cheerful.

   c. She had nothing to cry about.

2. Marygold was unhappy about the golden roses because they no longer had any ▭ .

   a. stems   b. petals   c. fragrance

3. Why couldn't Midas drink his tea?

   a. It was too hot.

   b. It had turned into gold.

   c. It was too bitter.

4. Why would Midas rather have had a real fish instead of a golden one?

   a. He was hungry.

   b. He liked the color.

   c. He wanted to see it wiggle.

5. After Midas began moving faster, he tried to eat a ▭ .

   a. potato   b. hotcake   c. fish

6. When that food was in his mouth, it ▭ .

   a. melted   b. turned cold

   c. burned his tongue

7. Why was Midas a person you should pity?

   a. He didn't have enough gold.

   b. He couldn't eat his breakfast.

   c. He lived in a palace.

8. After breakfast, what did Midas feel was worth the most?

   a. his daughter's love

   b. the Golden Touch

   c. a golden rose

B VOCABULARY

Complete each sentence with the correct word.

calculate	imitation	occupied
gleamed	inhale	ornament
grief	insane	wither

1. Flowers dry up when they

   _____ .

2. Haru paused to _____ the fragrance of the roses.

3. Sanjana tried to _____ how much water was in the bathtub.

4. Benito felt powerful _____ after his dog died.

5. Chapa could do a funny

   _____ of a duck quacking.

6. Harish painted a beautiful

   _____ inside the bowl.

7. The scientist was completely

   _____ by the difficult problem.

Copyright © McGraw-Hill Education

C MAPS

Work the items.

1. What sea is in the middle of the map?

   a. Caribbean   b. North

   c. Mediterranean

2. What is the name of country **A**?

   _____

3. What myth takes place in that country?

   _____

D COMPARISONS

Work the items.

1. When spectacles are changed into gold, you can't ▉ .

   a. put them on   b. see through them

   c. weigh them

2. When roses are changed into gold, you can't ▉ .

   a. smell them   b. touch them

   c. sell them

3. When a fish is changed into gold, you can't ▉ .

   a. hold it   b. eat it

   c. put it in water

GO TO PART D IN YOUR TEXTBOOK

Name ______________________________

A STORY DETAILS

Work the items.

1. Who told Midas how to get rid of the Golden Touch?
   a. Marygold b. his servants
   c. the stranger

2. To rid himself of the Golden Touch, Midas had to jump into ____ .
   a. a rose bush b. a pile of gold
   c. the river

3. To change objects back from gold to normal, Midas had to sprinkle them with ____ .
   a. river water b. gold dust
   c. rose petals

4. When Midas ran through the bushes, what season did his trail look like?
   a. spring b. summer c. fall

5. After Midas did what the stranger told him to do, he felt lighter because ____ .
   a. he took his shoes off
   b. his clothes were no longer gold
   c. the water held him up

6. What was the first thing that Midas changed back to normal?
   a. Marygold b. the roses
   c. his food

7. What **two** things always reminded Midas of the Golden Touch?
   a. the golden sunset
   b. the sands of the river
   c. Marygold's hair

8. With one exception, Midas ____ the sight of gold at the end of the story.
   a. loved b. hated
   c. had no feeling about

9. The exception was Marygold's golden ____________ .

B CHARACTER TRAITS

Complete each sentence with *Midas*, *Marygold*, or *The stranger*.

1. ____________________ was probably a god.
2. ____________________ learned a lesson about what's important in life.
3. ____________________ was the main character in "The Golden Touch."
4. ____________________ had brown hair that changed to golden hair.
5. ____________________ had a smile that made objects glow.
6. ____________________ could not see through his spectacles.

Complete each sentence with the correct word.

deceitful	envy	musician
deserved	frenzy	perpetual
dimple	linen	sincerely

1. The fancy office had a _____ clock on the bookshelf.

2. Some people think that men with a _____ on their chin are handsome.

3. The criminal was so _____ that no one trusted her.

4. The child _____ believed that the earth was flat.

5. Everybody clapped when the _____ walked onto the stage and got ready to play.

6. Midas learned that there's no reason to _____ people who are rich.

7. Midas got the punishment he _____ when he asked for the Golden Touch.

In the passage below, underline the sentence that tells the main theme of "The Golden Touch."

While Midas was feeling this terrible despair, he suddenly noticed somebody standing near the door. Midas bent down his head without speaking, for he recognized the figure as the stranger who had appeared the day before in the treasure room. The stranger's smile seemed to shed a yellow light all around the room. It gleamed on little Marygold's image and on the other objects that had been changed by the touch of Midas.

"Well, friend Midas," said the stranger, "how do you like the Golden Touch?"

Midas shook his head. "I am very miserable," he said.

"Very miserable? Indeed!" exclaimed the stranger. "And why is that? Have I not faithfully kept my promise to you? Didn't you get everything your heart desired?"

"Gold is not everything," answered Midas. "And I have lost all that my heart really cared for."

"Ah, so you have made a discovery since yesterday," observed the stranger.

GO TO PART D IN YOUR TEXTBOOK

A STORY DETAILS

Work the items.

1. The TV dance show that ran from 1952 to 1989 was called "American _____ ."

2. The band that Fausto saw on TV was called Los _____ .

3. Fausto's ▮▮▮▮ in life was to become a musician.

   a. permission   b. commission

   c. mission

4. The last album Fausto's parents bought was *The* _____ *Sing Christmas Favorites.*

5. Fausto's mother was making ▮▮▮▮ .

   a. tortillas   b. empanadas

   c. conjuntos

6. The dog Fausto found was named _____ .

7. Fausto planned to take the dog to its home and collect ▮▮▮▮ .

   a. an award   b. a fine

   c. a reward

8. The people who owned the dog had a ▮▮▮▮ clock.

   a. wind-up   b. battery-powered

   c. perpetual

B VOCABULARY

Complete each sentence with the correct word.

deceitful	muscular	sincerely
dimple	musician	stash
freeway	pew	warehouseman

1. The _____ lifted and moved boxes for his job.

2. The body builder showed off her _____ arms.

3. The robbers decided to _____ the gold in the basement.

4. Someone who lies is _____ and not to be trusted.

5. The driver decided to take the _____ because the streets were too crowded.

6. After entering the church, Lina sat down on a _____ .

7. It takes a lot of practice to become a good _____ .

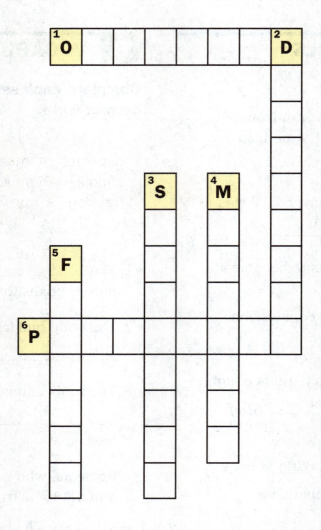

C CROSSWORD PUZZLE

Use the clues to complete the puzzle in CAPITAL LETTERS.

ACROSS

1. When you are busy, you are ▨ .

6. A ▨ clock is an expensive type of clock that can run without electricity and doesn't need to be wound up.

DOWN

2. When you deceive somebody by telling a lie, you are being ▨ .

3. Another word for *honestly* is ▨ .

4. When a body part has strong muscles, it is ▨ .

5. A free highway with many lanes of traffic is called a ▨ .

GO TO PART F IN YOUR TEXTBOOK

A STORY DETAILS

Work the items.

1. Before Fausto went to church, he ate *chorizo con* ▨ .

   a. *empanadas*   b. *enchiladas*

   c. *huevos*

2. The church service Fausto attended was called ▨ .

   a. confession   b. baptism

   c. mass

3. Father Jerry said that we are all ▨ .

   a. sinners   b. perfect

   c. faultless

4. During the service, Fausto said a Hail _____ prayer.

5. Fausto dropped a _____ -dollar bill into the wicker basket.

6. Later, Fausto tossed a grimy _____ into the wicker basket.

7. Instead of a guitar, Fausto got a _____ .

8. That instrument made a ▨ sound than a guitar.

   a. softer   b. deeper

   c. higher

B VOCABULARY

Complete each sentence with the correct word.

chorizo	enchiladas	huevo
conjunto	familia	lobo
empanadas	hijo	papas

1. The Spanish word for *egg* is _____ .

2. A type of Spanish sausage is _____ .

3. In Spanish, a son is called an _____ .

4. A Spanish word that looks almost the same as *family* is _____ .

5. Fausto's parents listened to _____ music.

6. Felipe rolled tortillas to make _____ .

7. The Spanish word for *wolf* is _____ .

C VOCABULARY

Complete each sentence with the correct word.

bass	mimic	resound
confession	muscular	stash
lector	pew	wicker

1. During the mass, the _____ told people about church events.

2. The band needed a low instrument, so they added a _____ guitar.

3. It's not nice to _____ the way someone talks.

4. The man knew he had sinned, so he went to _____ .

5. A clanging bell can _____ all over a village.

6. Zina used twigs from a willow tree to make a _____ chair.

7. The robber planned to _____ his loot in a dark forest.

D POINT OF VIEW

Complete each sentence with *first* or *third*.

1. In _____ -person narration, the narrator is a character in the story.

2. Except when characters are talking, a story in _____ -person narration doesn't use words like *I, me, we,* or *us.*

3. "The No-Guitar Blues" uses _____ -person narration.

4. "The Circuit" uses _____ -person narration.

5. "The Golden Touch" uses _____ -person narration.

6. In _____ -person narration, the narrator is not a character in the story.

GO TO PART F IN YOUR TEXTBOOK

A STORY DETAILS

Work the items.

1. The Olympian deities live on Mount

   _____ .

2. How many Olympian deities were there?

   a. six   b. nine   c. twelve

3. How many of the Olympian deities were

   women? _____

4. Which deity saw and knew everything?

   a. Aphrodite   b. Ares   c. Hermes

   d. Poseidon   e. Zeus

5. Which deity wore winged sandals?

   a. Aphrodite   b. Ares   c. Hermes

   d. Poseidon   e. Zeus

6. Which deity was the god of horses?

   a. Aphrodite   b. Ares   c. Hermes

   d. Poseidon   e. Zeus

7. Which deity wore a helmet and carried
   a spear?

   a. Aphrodite   b. Ares   c. Hermes

   d. Poseidon   e. Zeus

8. Goddesses and women envied ▮
   because she was beautiful.

   a. Aphrodite   b. Artemis

   c. Athena   d. Demeter

   e. Hera   f. Hestia

9. Hades ruled the _____ .

B VOCABULARY

Complete each sentence with the correct word.

bass	conquer	mimic
chariot	deity	miraculous
confession	disguise	wisdom

1. The soldiers used cannons to

   _____ the fort.

2. The queen rode around in a

   _____ pulled by white
   horses.

3. Athena was a Greek _____ .

4. At Halloween, many children are in

   _____ .

5. To play really low on a trombone, you

   need a _____ trombone.

6. Even though snow covered the ground,

   the _____ flowers
   bloomed.

7. People think that owls have lots of

   _____ , but the truth is that
   owls aren't very smart.

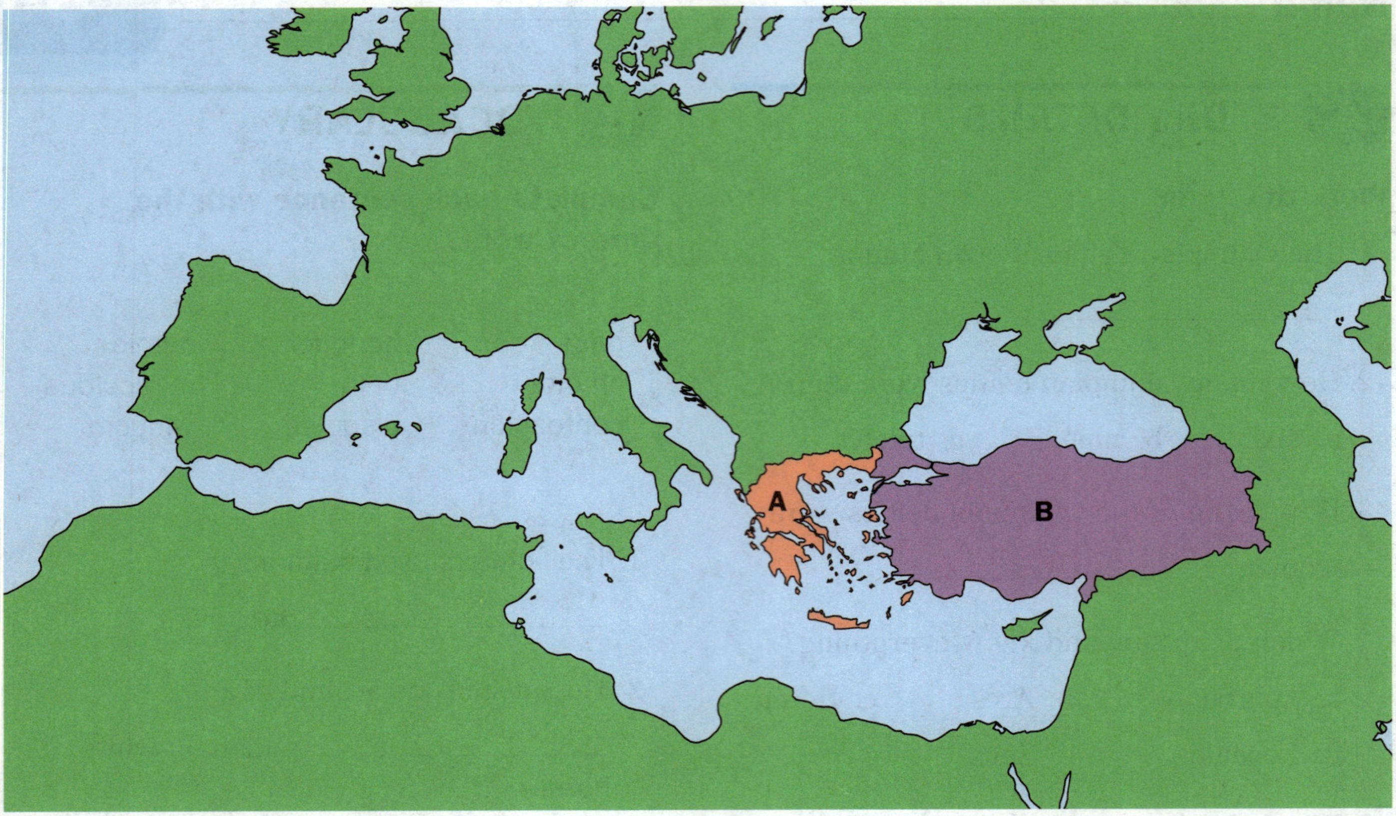

C MAPS

Work the items.

1. What is the name of country A?

   ____

2. What is the name of country B?

   ____

3. The ▬ Sea borders both country A and country B.

   a. Black b. Mediterranean

   c. North

4. The ▬ Sea runs along the northern border of country B.

   a. Black b. Mediterranean

   c. North

D CHARACTER TRAITS

Complete each sentence with *Aphrodite, Apollo, Ares, Demeter, Hades, Hermes, Poseidon,* or *Zeus.*

1. ____________________ was the deity of travelers.

2. ____________________ was the deity of love.

3. ____________________ was the deity of the sky.

4. ____________________ was the deity of the underworld.

5. ____________________ was the deity of the ocean.

6. ____________________ was the deity of war.

GO TO PART D IN YOUR TEXTBOOK

A STORY DETAILS

Work the items.

1. Baucis and Philemon were ▭ .

   a. young   b. middle-aged

   c. old

2. Baucis and Philemon had to work hard for a living because they were ▭ .

   a. poor   b. rich   c. slaves

3. Who would Baucis and Philemon treat better, their guests or themselves?

   _____

4. Long ago, the village near their valley had been a _____ .

5. The people who lived in the village were ▭ .

   a. kind   b. mean   c. unselfish

6. What would their children do to strangers?

   a. greet them warmly

   b. pelt them with stones

   c. run away from the strangers

7. Two _____ , carved in the wood, curled around the younger traveler's staff.

8. Near the top of the staff was a pair of _____ .

9. The younger traveler was wearing a ▭ cap that stuck out over both ears.

   a. round   b. triangular

   c. square

B VOCABULARY

Complete each sentence with the correct word.

chariot	deity	staff
conquer	fertile	stately
cultivate	hospitality	sympathy

1. Zeus was an Olympian _____ .

2. Two horses pulled the wooden _____ .

3. The army tried to _____ the city, but they failed.

4. When you are friendly and welcoming to somebody, you show _____ to that person.

5. The hiker used a long _____ carved from an oak branch.

6. Fruits and vegetables grew well in the _____ valley.

7. You need water and lots of time to _____ a garden.

C CHARACTER TRAITS

**Complete each sentence with *Philemon,
The younger traveler, or A village child.***

1. _____ has
   strange shoes.

2. _____ would
   give food to a stranger.

3. _____ threw
   stones at the strangers.

4. _____ would
   do anything for a guest.

5. _____ worked
   in his garden all day long.

6. _____ had
   feet that seemed to rise above the ground.

D GREEK GODDESSES

**Complete each sentence with the
correct name.**

Aphrodite	Athena	Hera
Artemis	Demeter	Hestia

1. The goddess of wisdom was

   _____ .

2. The goddess of love was

   _____ .

3. The goddess of hunting was

   _____ .

4. The goddess of farming was

   _____ .

E GREEK GODS

**Complete each sentence with the
correct name.**

Apollo	Hephaestus	Poseidon
Ares	Hermes	Zeus

1. The god of travelers was

   _____ .

2. The god of war was

   _____ .

3. The god of the sky was

   _____ .

4. The god of the ocean was

   _____ .

GO TO PART D IN YOUR TEXTBOOK

A STORY DETAILS

Work the items.

1. When the older stranger frowned, the twilight seemed to grow ▨ .

    a. lighter   b. taller   c. darker

2. Philemon thought the older stranger was ▨ .

    a. stupid   b. ordinary   c. wise

3. What was the farthest distance Philemon had ever been from his cottage?

    a. ten miles   b. twenty miles

    c. fifty miles

4. Who did Philemon want to die together with?

    a. Quicksilver   b. Baucis

    c. nobody

5. Quicksilver was always ▨ .

    a. smiling   b. frowning

    c. shouting

6. Quicksilver's staff got into the cottage by ▨ .

    a. dragging itself along the ground

    b. hopping and fluttering

    c. flying high in the air

7. What part of the staff made it move?

    a. the wings   b. the snakes

    c. the bottom tip

8. After Baucis poured milk for the strangers, she saw that the pitcher was ▨ .

    a. half full   b. almost empty

    c. empty

B CHARACTER TRAITS

Complete each sentence with *Baucis, Quicksilver,* or *The older stranger.*

1. _____ made butter and cheese.

2. _____ looked very wise.

3. _____ had a deep voice.

4. _____ was light-footed.

5. _____ was always smiling.

6. _____ was worried about the amount of food.

7. _____ had a staff.

8. _____ wanted to die at the same time as someone else.

C VOCABULARY

Complete each sentence with the correct word.

apology	fertile	talkative
cultivate	miraculous	wisdom
disguise	shrewd	witty

1. Felipe was so _____ that he could chat for hours.

2. Someone who has been around the world and thought deeply has

   _____ .

3. Imena was mean to Mario, so she had to

   give him an _____ .

4. The pitcher seemed _____ because it filled up with milk all by itself.

5. The pitcher made a _____ move by throwing a curveball.

6. For a good vegetable garden, you need to

   start with _____ soil.

7. Rento though he was

   _____ , but nobody laughed at his stupid jokes.

GO TO PART D IN YOUR TEXTBOOK

A STORY DETAILS

Work the items.

1. Which Olympian deity is most likely to be Quicksilver?

   a. Ares   b. Hermes   c. Apollo

2. Which Olympian deity is most likely to be the older traveler?

   a. Hades   b. Poseidon   c. Zeus

3. What came out of the empty pitcher when Baucis poured Quicksilver a second cup?

   _____

4. Baucis was surprised when the _____ became light and moist.

5. Each grape was nearly bursting with ripe _____ .

6. Philemon saw a little white fountain of milk at the bottom of ▮ .

   a. Quicksilver's cup

   b. the older traveler's cup

   c. the pitcher

7. Quicksilver said that his _____ had charmed the pitcher.

8. Baucis and Philemon slept ▮ that night.

   a. in their bed   b. on the floor

   c. outside

9. The next morning, what couldn't Quicksilver see?

   a. the village   b. the cottage

   c. the older traveler

B VOCABULARY

Complete each sentence with the correct word.

abundant	hospitality	spacious
astonishment	inhabitant	stately
disagreeable	preparations	sympathy

1. Somebody who lives in a place is an _____ of that place.

2. Another word for *amazement* is _____ .

3. When you prepare for something, you make _____ .

4. When you are unfriendly and unpleasant, you are _____ .

5. When there's a lot of something, that thing is _____ .

6. A building with lots of space inside is a _____ building.

7. A tree that is big and impressive is a _____ tree.

C CHARACTER TRAITS

Complete each sentence with *A villager,* *Baucis,* or *Quicksilver.*

1. _____ throws stones at a stranger.

2. _____ tries to make a weary traveler comfortable.

3. _____ refuses to give a traveler a glass of water.

4. _____ has a magic staff.

5. _____ only sells bread to poor people.

6. _____ gives a poor person something to eat for free.

D CLASSIFICATION

Complete each sentence with *hunting,* *food,* or *carrying.*

1. People use cats mainly for
_____ .

2. People use donkeys mainly for
_____ .

3. People use goats mainly for
_____ .

4. People use llamas mainly for
_____ .

5. People use chickens mainly for
_____ .

E TIMELINES

Write the correct event from Jackie Robinson's life after each date on the timeline.

- Jackie helps win the World Series.
- Jackie dies.
- Jackie first plays for the Dodgers.
- Jackie leaves UCLA.

1972 _____

_____

1955 _____

_____

1947 _____

_____

1941 _____

_____

GO TO PART D IN YOUR TEXTBOOK

A STORY DETAILS

Work the items.

1. Baucis and Philemon saw that the village and the valley had been turned into a

   _____ .

2. The villagers had been changed into

   _____ .

3. What did Baucis and Philemon say they wanted most in the world?

   a. to live forever

   b. to live and die together

   c. to have a palace

4. Baucis and Philemon's cottage was turned into a marble _____ .

5. Milk from the miraculous pitcher tasted _____ to friendly guests.

6. Milk from the miraculous pitcher tasted _____ to disagreeable guests.

7. After they died, Baucis and Philemon were changed into two _____ .

8. What did somebody build around those objects?

   a. a palace courtyard

   b. a circular seat

   c. a fence

9. What kind of people would sit there?

   a. travelers   b. kings and queens

   c. deities

B VOCABULARY

Complete each sentence with the correct word.

abundant	device	predicted
astonishment	disagreeable	preparations
decay	inhabitant	substance

1. Trang's teeth began to

   _____ because he ate too much candy.

2. Grease is a thick and slippery

   _____ .

3. Juanita lived in Houston, so she was an

   _____ of Houston.

4. Arka invented a _____ that turned pages.

5. Eva looked at the gray sky and

   _____ that it would rain.

6. Apples were so _____ that people got tired of eating them.

7. The night before his trip, Justin made

   _____ .

C ROMAN DEITIES

Complete each sentence with *Mercury, Venus, Mars, Jupiter,* or *Neptune.*

1. _____ is the Roman god of the sky.

2. _____ is the Roman god of the ocean.

3. _____ is the Roman goddess of love.

4. _____ is sometimes called Quicksilver.

5. _____ is the Roman god of war.

6. _____ is the Roman god of travelers.

D RELATED WORDS

After each word, write a related word that begins or ends with *atmos, geo, hydro, izer,* or *ous.*

1. fertile _____

2. thermal _____

3. mischief _____

4. electric _____

5. sphere _____

E PLANET NAMES

Complete each sentence with the name of a planet.

1. _____ is the planet that's closest to the sun.

2. _____ is named after the Roman god of war.

3. _____ is the third planet from the sun.

4. _____ is named after the Roman goddess of love.

5. _____ is the dwarf planet that's farthest from the sun.

6. _____ is named after the Roman god of the sky.

GO TO PART E IN YOUR TEXTBOOK

A   STORY DETAILS

Work the items.

1. Which of the following are fossil fuels?

   a. coal   b. sunlight   c. wind

   d. gas   e. water   f. oil

2. When fossil fuels burn, they release

   _____ dioxide and other
   pollutants into the atmosphere.

3. The process that's heating up the Earth is

   called _____ warming.

4. Peat forms at the bottom of

   _____ .

5. After millions of years, peat turns into

   _____ .

6. Which types of vehicles reduce pollution?

   a. gasoline-powered cars   b. bicycles

   c. trains   d. subways

   e. diesel trucks   f. buses

7. A renewable fuel made from corn is called

   _____ .

8. Power from the sun is called

   _____ power.

9. Electricity from dams is called

   _____ power.

B   VOCABULARY

Complete each sentence with the correct word.

carbon	generator	nonrenewable
diesel	inexhaustible	resources
fossil	microscope	turbine

1. Oil, gas, wind, and water are examples of

   energy _____ .

2. Fuels made from the remains of living

   things are called _____
   fuels.

3. Fuels that can't be renewed are called

   _____ fuels.

4. Sun, wind, and water are

   _____ sources of energy.

5. Fuel that is dirtier than gasoline is called

   _____ fuel.

6. Rushing water in a dam spins a

   _____ around and around.

7. A machine that turns spinning energy into

   electricity is called a _____ .

C PLANET NAMES

Complete each sentence.

1. The planet Mars is named after the Roman

   god of _____ .

2. The planet Jupiter is named after the

   Roman god of the _____ .

3. The planet Venus is named after the

   Roman goddess of _____ .

4. The planet Mercury is named after the

   Roman god of _____ .

5. The dwarf planet Pluto is named after the

   Roman god of the _____ .

6. The planet Neptune is named after the

   Roman god of the _____ .

D RELATED WORDS

After each word, write a related word that begins with one of the word parts in the box.

atmos	hydro	micro
geo	in	non

1. renewable _____

2. thermal _____

3. exhaustible _____

4. electric _____

5. scope _____

GO TO PART D IN YOUR TEXTBOOK

A STORY DETAILS

Work the items.

1. The number of children in the merchant's family was _____ .

2. One day their house caught _____ and burned to the ground.

3. The family moved into a ▨ one hundred miles from the town.

   a. mansion   b. cottage   c. barn

4. Beauty asked her father to bring her a _____ .

5. Beauty's sisters asked their father to bring them _____ and dresses.

6. After the merchant reached the town, he discovered that he was _____ than when he had left the cottage.

7. On the way home, the merchant slept in the _____ trunk of a tree.

8. The trees the merchant found were covered with

   _____

   _____ .

9. What began to terrify the merchant at the end of the chapter?

   a. the silence   b. the Beast

   c. rumbling sounds

B VOCABULARY

Complete each sentence with the correct word.

carbon	fatigue	persuade
cautious	fossil	terrify
desolate	generator	turbine

1. Justin tried to _____ his mother to let him stay out late on a school night.

2. Zoo workers have to be _____ when they enter lion cages.

3. Cars pollute the air by making _____ dioxide.

4. The North Pole is a _____ place far from any town.

5. A device with blades that spin around and around is called a _____ .

6. The growling bear began to _____ the frightened campers.

C SEQUENCING

Number the events in the correct sequence.

_____ The merchant found a palace.

_____ The merchant spent the night in a tree.

_____ The merchant moved to a cottage.

_____ The merchant's house burned down.

_____ The merchant went back to the town.

D RELATED FACTS

Complete each sentence with *Hermes, Hades, Poseidon, Zeus,* or *Ares.*

1. _____ was the Greek god of the sky.

2. _____ carried a staff with wings.

3. _____ was the Greek god of the ocean.

4. _____ was the Greek god of travelers.

5. _____ was a Greek god who lived underground.

6. _____ was the brother of the Greek goddess of love.

E STORY REVIEW

Write which story or biography each item describes.

1. Zeus and Hermes appear in this story.

   _____

2. This story is a folktale.

   _____

3. The main character in this story is a king who lives in Turkey.

   _____

4. The subject of this biography was a baseball player.

   _____

5. The main character in this story wants to get a guitar.

   _____

6. The main character in this story tells the story himself.

   _____

GO TO PART E IN YOUR TEXTBOOK

Name ______________________________ 93

A STORY DETAILS

Work the items.

1. Although the season was __________ everywhere else, the Beast's garden was warm and sunny.

2. The merchant remembered his promise to Beauty, so he picked a __________ for her.

3. The Beast said he would let the merchant live if the merchant gave him one of his __________.

4. The Beast allowed the merchant to return home for one _____.

   a. day   b. week   c. month

5. If the merchant did not return after that time, the Beast would _____.

   a. kidnap one of the merchant's daughters
   b. come and get the merchant
   c. kill the merchant's family

6. The merchant's children thought his journey had gone well when they saw the splendid __________.

7. The only child to receive a gift from the merchant was __________.

8. The other children began to make plans for __________ the Beast.

9. The other daughters were angry with Beauty because _____.

   a. her request had caused all the trouble
   b. she was the youngest
   c. they wanted her rose

B CHARACTER TRAITS

Complete each sentence with *The merchant, The Beast, Beauty,* or *Beauty's sisters.*

1. __________ wanted jewels and dresses.
2. __________ asked for a rose.
3. __________ agreed to let somebody take his place.
4. __________ always tried to make the best of things.
5. __________ looked ugly.
6. __________ picked a rose for somebody else.
7. __________ lived all alone in a palace.
8. __________ agreed to take somebody's place.

Copyright © McGraw-Hill Education

C — VOCABULARY

Complete each sentence with the correct word.

bid	distressed	persuade
cautious	fatigue	soothe
desolate	hasty	terrify

1. The father tried to _____ his baby daughter by singing to her.

2. The baby was so _____ by her father's out-of-tune singing that she began to wail.

3. The father made a _____ decision to stop singing immediately.

4. The father decided to use another method to _____ the baby to stop wailing.

5. It was almost nap time, and the baby was showing signs of _____ .

6. The father put the baby in her crib and _____ it goodbye.

7. The father was so _____ when he closed the door that it didn't make any noise.

D — GREEK DEITIES

Complete each sentence with Hermes, Poseidon, Zeus, Ares, Aphrodite, or Hades.

1. _____ was the god of the ocean.

2. _____ was the god of the sky.

3. _____ was the god of travelers.

4. _____ commanded thunder and lightning.

5. _____ was the goddess of love.

6. _____ lived in the underworld.

7. _____ was the god of war.

GO TO PART D IN YOUR TEXTBOOK

A STORY DETAILS

Work the items.

1. When Beauty and her father rode to the Beast's palace at night, why was the forest so light?

   a. The sun had come up.

   b. Colored lights were shining.

   c. The moon was full.

2. The air was bitterly cold before, but when the merchant and Beauty reached the palace, the air was _____ .

3. Beauty made a great effort to hide her _____ when she met the Beast.

4. The Beast was pleased that Beauty had come to the palace ▩ .

   a. reluctantly   b. blindfolded

   c. willingly

5. The more gold Beauty put into the trunks, the _____ room there seemed to be.

6. The merchant thought the Beast had deceived them because the trunks ▩ .

   a. were too small

   b. weighed so much

   c. wouldn't open

7. Beauty first saw the prince in a ▩ .

   a. dream   b. painting

   c. mirror

8. The prince told Beauty not to trust her _____ too much.

9. The prince asked Beauty not to desert him until she had saved him from his _____ .

B SETTINGS

Complete each sentence with *the forest, the palace,* or *her dream.*

1. Beauty saw a chest of gold in _____ .

2. Beauty saw fireworks in _____ .

3. Beauty saw a brook bordered with trees in _____ .

4. Beauty saw a little room with a fireplace in _____ .

5. Beauty saw colored lights in _____ .

6. Beauty saw a young prince in _____ .

7. Beauty saw cupboards full of jewels in _____ .

C VOCABULARY

Complete each sentence with the correct word.

> anxiety   dreaded   microscope
> bid   hasty   nonrenewable
> distressed   inexhaustible soothe

1. Ria was so worried that you could see the
   _____ on her face.

2. Marco couldn't swim, so he
   _____ going to the
   swimming pool.

3. When something can't be used up, it is
   _____ .

4. When vacation ended, Gina
   _____ her grandparents
   goodbye.

5. The scientist used a _____
   to see tiny living things in a drop of water.

6. The small cat was _____
   when it saw the big dog approaching.

7. Pedro's mother tried to
   _____ him after his team
   lost the big game.

D STORY REVIEW

Complete each item with:

- Adventure on the Rocky Ridge
- The Cat That Walked by Himself
- For the Love of a Man
- The Golden Touch
- A Horse to Remember
- The Miraculous Pitcher
- The Ugly Duckling

1. The main character in this story pulled a
   thousand-pound sled.

   _____

2. The main character in this story turned
   into a swan.

   _____

3. The main character in this story was a cat
   that could talk.

   _____

4. Hermes and Zeus appeared in this story.

   _____

5. This story showed how evil greed can be.

   _____

6. The main character in this story rode in a
   steeplechase.

   _____

7. Two of the characters in this story turned
   into trees.

   _____

GO TO PART D IN YOUR TEXTBOOK

A STORY DETAILS

Work the items.

1. Beauty found a bracelet with the prince's picture hanging from a

   _____ .

2. Beauty found a _____ of the prince in the room filled with pictures.

3. Every night, the Beast asked Beauty if she would _____ him.

4. Beauty's answer to the Beast's question was always, "_____ ."

5. Beauty's answer made the Beast feel

   _____ .

6. Beauty agreed to visit her family for two

   _____ .

7. The Beast said if Beauty did not come back in time, he would

   _____ .

8. Beauty could get back to the palace by turning a _____ .

9. Beauty said that it was not the Beast's fault that he was so _____ .

B VOCABULARY

Complete each sentence with the correct word.

anxiety	diesel	resources
chandelier	dread	
conceal	portraits	

1. The fancy dining room had a

   _____ with twelve lights hanging over the middle of the table.

2. The artist earned her living by painting

   _____ of rich and famous people.

3. Some big trucks burn

   _____ fuel, which is quite smoky.

4. When you are worried and nervous, you feel _____ .

5. Fossil fuels and solar power are examples of energy _____ .

6. Children often _____ getting their hair cut.

7. The students posed for classroom

   _____ .

C ROMAN DEITIES

Complete each sentence with *Mercury, Venus, Mars, Jupiter, Neptune,* or *Pluto.*

1. _____ was the Roman god of the underworld.

2. _____ was the Roman god of the sky.

3. _____ was the Roman goddess of love.

4. _____ was the Roman god of the sea.

5. _____ was the Roman god of war.

GO TO PART D IN YOUR TEXTBOOK

Name _____

A STORY DETAILS

Work the items.

1. Beauty's _____ had grown used to being without her.

2. The merchant told Beauty, "I think the prince wants you to marry the Beast _____ his ugliness."

3. On the night that Beauty was supposed to return to the palace, she had a ▢ dream.

   a. dismal   b. pleasant   c. boring

4. In her dream, Beauty found the Beast in a _____ .

5. In Beauty's dream, the Beast was ▢ .

   a. sleeping   b. dying

   c. wounded

6. After Beauty returned to the palace, she could not find a _____ of the Beast in the garden.

7. The Beast woke up when Beauty sprinkled _____ on his face.

8. In the cave, Beauty told the Beast, "I never knew how much I _____ you until now, when I feared I was too late to save your life."

9. When Beauty agreed to marry the Beast, he turned into the _____ .

B VOCABULARY

Complete each sentence with the correct word.

appearances	despite	predict
chandelier	furthermore	spell
conceal	portraits	trace

1. He put a _____ on her, and she couldn't get him out of her mind.

2. When people grow up, they learn not to be fooled by _____ .

3. In the ghost story, the house suddenly vanished without leaving a _____ .

4. Rembrandt was a painter who is famous for painting _____ of himself.

5. The robber tried to _____ the stolen candlesticks under his coat.

6. Odina is an excellent student; _____ , she's a great athlete.

7. The children played outside _____ the heavy rain.

Copyright © McGraw-Hill Education

C SEQUENCING

Number the events in the correct sequence.

_____ The merchant met the Beast.

_____ Beauty married the prince.

_____ The merchant lost all his money.

_____ Beauty agreed to go to the Beast's palace.

_____ Beauty had her first dream about the prince.

D STORY REVIEW

Complete each item with the title of a story you have read.

1. This realistic story is about migrant workers in California.

   _____

2. This myth takes place in Turkey.

   _____

3. This story is a French folktale.

   _____

4. This realistic story takes place in North Carolina.

   _____

5. This Greek myth involves two deities.

   _____

6. This realistic story takes place in Fresno, California during the 1980s.

   _____

GO TO PART D IN YOUR TEXTBOOK

A STORY DETAILS

Work the items.

1. "The Bracelet" is an example of

   _____ -person narration.

2. On December 7, 1941, the Japanese
   attacked the U.S. Navy base at

   _____ Harbor, in the state

   of _____ .

3. According to President Roosevelt,
   Japanese Americans were sent to

   _____ camps, but Ruri calls

   them _____ camps.

4. The letters POW stand for

   _____

   _____

   _____ .

5. Ruri lives in the city of

   _____ in the state of

   _____ .

6. Ruri compares her house to an empty

   _____ box that has a lot of

   _____ .

7. Ruri hopes that a messenger at her door

   will have a _____ from
   her father.

8. Ruri's mother packed the dishes,
   blankets, and sheets into an

   enormous _____ bag.

9. Laurie gave Ruri a _____

   that was made of _____

   and had a _____ dangling
   from it.

B VOCABULARY

Complete each sentence with the correct word.

alien	despite	interned
appearance	duffel	telegram
concentration	evacuate	trace

1. Someone from another country is an

   _____ until he or she
   becomes a citizen.

2. People were ordered to

   _____ the city because the
   air was poisonous.

3. Before email and text messaging, the
   fastest way to send a written message was

   the _____ .

4. The magician seems to vanish from the

   stage without a _____ .

5. The boat kept sailing _____
   the high winds.

6. It's not a good idea to put breakable items

   in a _____ bag.

7. The horses were _____ in
   the barn during the night.

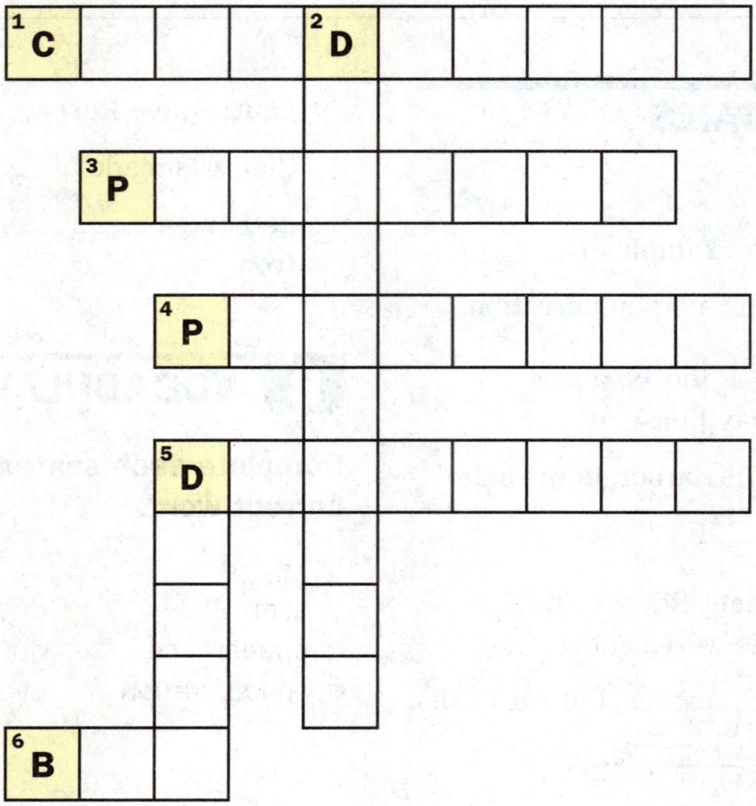

C CROSSWORD PUZZLE

Use CAPITAL LETTERS to complete the puzzle.

ACROSS

1. A fancy light with branches that hangs from the ceiling is called a ____ .
3. Another word for *convince* is ____ .
4. A painting, photo, or drawing of a person is called a ____ .
5. Another word for *bleak* is ____ .
6. When you say goodbye to somebody, you ____ them farewell.

DOWN

2. When you feel great sorrow or pain, you are ____ .
5. When you fear something, you ____ it.

GO TO PART E IN YOUR TEXTBOOK

A STORY DETAILS

Work the items.

1. The Civil Control Station was located in the ▨ church.

   a. Catholic   b. Congregational

   c. Conversational

2. The flowers beside the fish pond were called _____ .

3. The first camp Ruri went to was at the _____ Racetracks.

4. The sign on the boarded-up store said, "We are _____ Americans."

5. Ruri's apartment was in a horse _____ in a long stable.

6. The apartment had three Army ▨ for sleeping.

   a. caughts   b. hammocks   c. cots

7. Ruri had promised _____ that she would never take off the bracelet.

8. The second camp Ruri went to was called _____ , in the state of _____ .

9. Mama said, "Those are things we can carry in our _____ and take with us no matter where we are sent."

B VOCABULARY

Complete each sentence with the correct word.

bayonet	interned	radishes
bean-curd	loomed	register
evacuate	mental	telegram

1. You can't take swimming lessons until you _____ at the swimming pool office.

2. The Japanese restaurant served _____ cake.

3. The soldier's rifle stopped working, so he began using his _____ .

4. Suddenly, the giant monster _____ up from the ground.

5. The POWs were _____ in a camp surrounded by a high fence with guard towers.

6. The cook pickled the _____ in special vinegar with secret spices.

7. Solving puzzles takes a lot of _____ activity.

How Pazi Spends Her Time on School Days

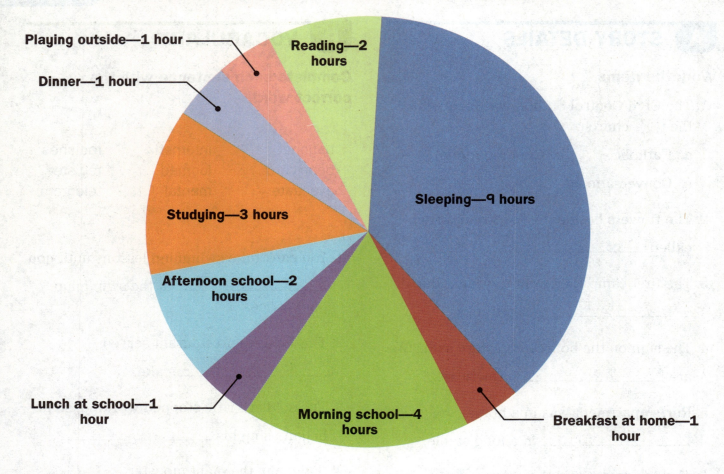

Playing outside—1 hour
Dinner—1 hour
Reading—2 hours
Sleeping—9 hours
Studying—3 hours
Afternoon school—2 hours
Lunch at school—1 hour
Morning school—4 hours
Breakfast at home—1 hour

C CHARTS AND GRAPHS

Work the items.

1. How many hours does Pazi spend in school on school days?
   _____

2. On which activity does Pazi spend the most time? _____

3. How many hours a day does Pazi spend on meals? _____

4. How many hours a day does Pazi spend on all her activities? _____

5. Which is longer: *morning school* or *afternoon school*?
   _____

6. On which activity does Pazi spend the least time: *playing*, *reading*, or *studying*?
   _____

GO TO PART D IN YOUR TEXTBOOK

A STORY DETAILS

Work the items.

1. At the beginning of the poem, the fly invites the spider to walk into his ▇▇▇ .

   a. pallor   b. parlor   c. parley

2. The "winding stair" the spider refers to is actually his

   _____ .

3. The fly says that asking her to go up the

   winding stair is in _____ .

4. The "pretty curtains" and "fine and thin" sheets the spider mentions are ▇▇▇ .

   a. silk   b. lace   c. webbing

5. The fly says that animals who sleep on the spider's bed never, never

   _____ again.

6. The spider says he has good food in his ▇▇▇ .

   a. entry   b. pantry   c. eatery

7. The spider compares the fly's wings to a

   _____ .

8. The spider says he has a

   _____ -glass on his parlor shelf.

9. When the spider says "behold yourself," he means ▇▇▇ .

   a. look at yourself

   b. hold onto yourself

   c. dig a hole into yourself

B VOCABULARY

Complete each sentence with the correct word.

bayonet	pantry	register
loomed	parlor	vain
mental	pearly	weary

1. The family tried in _____ to keep their dog from barking.

2. The restaurant stored its food in a large

   _____ .

3. The guests sat down in the

   _____ and began talking.

4. Giant thunder clouds suddenly

   _____ up on the horizon.

5. Hama was so _____ after her soccer game that she collapsed into bed.

6. You need to _____ for some websites before you can use them.

7. Mert was so proud of his

   _____ teeth that he brushed them three times a day.

C POEM STRUCTURE

Work the items.

1. Fill in the blanks in the stanza below.

   "Sweet creature," said the spider, "you're witty and you're wise,

   How handsome are your pearly wings, how brilliant are your _____ !

   I have a little looking-glass upon my parlor shelf,

   If you'll step in one moment, dear, you shall behold _____ ."

   "I thank you, gentle sir," she said, "for what you're pleased to say,

   And bidding you good morning now, I'll call another _____ ."

2. A pair of lines in poetry is called a ▨ .

   a. couple   b. coupling

   c. couplet

3. A pair of lines that rhyme is called a

   _____

   _____ .

4. The rhyme scheme for the stanza above is ▨ .

   a. ABABCC   b. ABCABC

   c. AABBCC

D THEMES

For each story, write the letter of the theme.

A. All that glitters is not gold.

B. Be kind to strangers.

C. No matter where you go, you will always bring your memories.

D. Do not trust appearances.

E. Common things are more valuable than gold.

1. The Miraculous Pitcher ____

2. The Golden Touch ____

3. Beauty and the Beast ____

4. The Bracelet ____

GO TO PART D IN YOUR TEXTBOOK

A STORY DETAILS

Work the items.

1. In poetry, a pair of lines that rhyme is
   called a _____
   _____ .

2. In poetry, a group of two or more lines is
   called a _____ .

3. A spider web that is delicate and clever is
   a _____ web.

4. When the spider in the poem wants the fly
   to come back to his web, he tells her,
   "Come _____ ."

5. The spider tells the fly that her wing is
   _____ and silver.

6. The spider tells the fly that her
   _____ are green
   and purple.

7. The spider tells the fly that her eyes are
   like the _____ bright, but
   his are dull as _____ .

8. What does "She hung aloft" mean?

   a. She hung around in a loft.

   b. She spun around.

   c. She stayed in the air.

9. The contraction of the word *never* is
   _____ .

B VOCABULARY

**Complete each sentence with the
correct word.**

alas	flit	hue
aloft	heed	idle
crest	hither	unto

1. The helicopter stayed
   _____ , just under
   the clouds.

2. José wanted to buy a green car, but his wife
   wanted another _____ .

3. If you come _____ , I can
   show you the stain in the rug.

4. The blue jay has a blue
   _____ on top of its head.

5. Zina's speech was filled with
   _____ words that
   meant nothing.

6. The goat refused to _____
   the farmer's commands.

7. Bees _____ from plant to
   plant, looking for nectar.

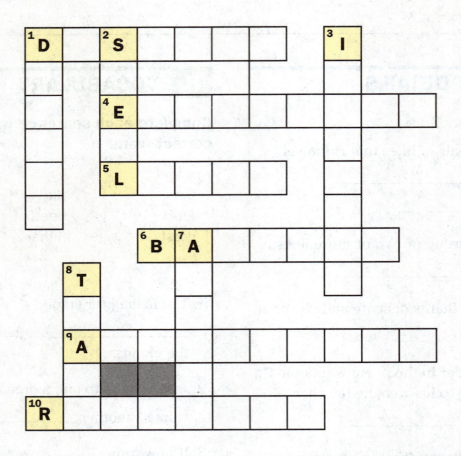

C CROSSWORD PUZZLE

Use CAPITAL LETTERS to complete the puzzle.

ACROSS

1. When you do something even though you have a problem, you do that thing ___ your problem.

4. When the government forces people to leave an area, the government ___ the area.

5. When something really big appears, it ___ up.

6. A ___ is a sharp metal blade that can be attached to the end of a rifle.

9. The way something looks is called its ___ .

10. When you sign up for something, you ___ for that thing.

DOWN

1. A ___ bag is a type of suitcase.

2. A magic charm is called a ___ .

3. When you are ___ in a place, you are not allowed to leave that place.

7. People from another country are sometimes called ___ .

8. A clue that something has been somewhere is called a ___ .

GO TO PART E IN YOUR TEXTBOOK

A   STORY DETAILS

Work the items.

1. The subject of this biography is Jane

   _____ .

2. That person lived in the city of

   _____ .

3. The street that is exactly one mile west of that city's downtown area is called

   _____ Street.

4. The museum on that street is called

   _____ House.

5. The narrators in the biography are ▮▮▮ people.

   a. real   b. fictional

6. The events the narrators tell about are ▮▮▮ events.

   a. real   b. fictional

7. The first narrator is named Maria

   _____ .

8. Maria's parents were from the country of

   _____ .

9. The language Maria's parents spoke was

   _____ .

B   VOCABULARY

Complete each line of the poem with the correct word.

alas	cunning	hue
aloft	flitting	idle
crested	hither	subtle

1. Alas, _____ ! how very soon this silly little fly,

2. Hearing the cunning, flattering words, came slowly _____ by;

3. With buzzing wings she hung _____ , then near and nearer drew,

4. Thinking only of her brilliant eyes, and green and purple _____ —

5. Thinking only of her _____ head—poor foolish thing! At last,

6. Up jumped the _____ spider, and fiercely held her fast.

C MAPS

Work the items.

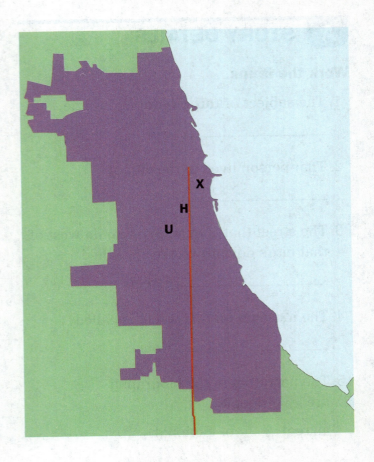

1. The purple area on the map shows the
   city of _____ .

2. The green area shows the [gray box] of
   that city.

   a. downtown   b. suburbs
   c. neighborhoods

3. The blue area shows Lake

   _____ .

4. The red line shows _____
   Street.

5. The U shows the _____
   of Illinois at _____ .

6. The H shows _____

   _____ .

GO TO PART D IN YOUR TEXTBOOK

A STORY DETAILS

Work the items.

1. The merchants who came down Maria's street were called ▓ .

   a. paddlers   b. peddlers

   c. puddlers

2. Circle **three** things those merchants sold.

   a. computers   b. ice

   c. vegetables   d. televisions

   e. coal   f. cell phones

3. Maria's family would go to Lake
   _____ for picnics.

4. Which direction was that lake from their house?

   a. north   b. south

   c. east   d. west

5. Who would Maria's mother argue with in the morning?

   a. Maria   b. Maria's father

   c. peddlers

6. On her way to work, Maria walked down
   _____ Street.

7. Maria worked in a _____ factory.

8. Which language was Maria not allowed to speak at work?

   _____

B VOCABULARY

Complete each sentence with the correct word.

foreman	pearly	weary
pantry	peddler	
parlor	purchase	

1. Gino went to the store to
   _____ a dozen eggs.

2. A room where food is stored is called
   a _____ .

3. At the factory, the _____ kept an eye on the workers in her group.

4. The children raced outside when they heard the ice cream _____ ringing the bells on his cart.

5. Prakash was so _____ after school that he fell asleep on the school bus.

6. At the party, people sat and talked in the
   _____ .

C STORY REVIEW

Work the items.

1. In the biography you are reading, Maria lives in the city of _____ .

2. The street exactly one mile west of that city's downtown is called _____ Street.

3. The name of the large house on that street was _____ House.

4. The neighborhoods around that house were ▓▓▓ .

   a. rich   b. poor   c. middle class

5. Maria's family came from the country of _____ .

D CLASSIFICATION

Write whether the main use of each animal is *hunting*, *food*, or *carrying*.

1. Elephant _____

2. Hound _____

3. Donkey _____

4. Sheep _____

5. Dog _____

6. Chicken _____

E RELATED FACTS

Work the items.

1. A baseball game lasts _____ innings if there's not a tie.

2. When a team is not batting, how many of its players are on the field? _____

3. The _____ stands between second and third base.

4. The person who calls balls and strikes is called the _____ .

5. The player who throws to the batter is called the _____ .

6. How many outs does each team get during an inning? _____

GO TO PART E IN YOUR TEXTBOOK

A STORY DETAILS

Work the items.

1. What would happen to Maria if she was one minute late for work?

    a. She would have to explain why she was late.

    b. She would lose one hour of pay.

    c. She would have to work an hour longer.

2. The _____ yelled at Maria if she stopped working for a moment.

3. Maria worked for _____ hours a day.

4. The two women who started Hull House were Jane _____ and Ellen _____ .

5. They wanted to turn the old Hull place into a ▭ house.

    a. suburban   b. customs

    c. settlement

6. The women started a free _____ for young children at Hull House.

7. What language were the women going to teach?

    _____

8. The women were also going to start classes in cooking and _____ .

9. Maria asked if she could bring her younger _____ to Hull House.

B SETTINGS

Complete each sentence with *Maria's neighborhood, the factory,* or *Hull House.*

1. There were boxes overflowing with garbage in

    _____ .

2. Maria saw expensive furniture inside

    _____ .

3. Young children could go to kindergarten inside _____ .

4. The smell was very sweet inside

    _____ .

5. Rats and insects were everywhere in

    _____ .

6. A foreman would yell when somebody stopped working in

    _____ .

C VOCABULARY

Complete each sentence with the correct word.

agile	foreman	purchase
carpenter	peddler	settlement

1. People lined up at the cash register to _____ their groceries.

2. The student learned how to be a _____ by cutting wood and nailing it together.

3. People in the neighborhood went to the _____ house when they needed help learning English.

4. The acrobat was so _____ that she could turn cartwheels anywhere.

5. It's hard to make money as a _____ if nobody buys your products.

D FACT AND FICTION

Write whether each statement is *fact* or *fiction*.

1. There are twelve deities who live on Mount Olympus. _____

2. The Greeks believed that deities lived on Mount Olympus. _____

3. Monkeys have wings and can fly through the air. _____

4. A witch can turn a prince into a frog. _____

5. A man can have an insane desire for gold. _____

GO TO PART D IN YOUR TEXTBOOK

A STORY DETAILS

Work the items.

1. Maria said that _____ was the most beautiful season in her neighborhood.

2. During the winter, Maria's family covered their windows with old

   _____ so the heat would not escape.

3. The candy factory closed down because

   the _____ system broke.

4. One evening, Maria and her friends went to Hull House to practice

   _____ .

5. The first owner of the dress Maria wore

   on Sunday was her _____ .

6. After she put on her dress, Maria draped a

   _____ around her shoulders.

7. Why didn't Maria want anybody to look at her feet?

   a. She didn't have any shoes.

   b. Her shoes had holes in them.

   c. She wasn't wearing socks.

8. After the concert, Jane Addams offered

   the girls hard _____ .

9. The law passed in 1893 made it illegal for

   children under _____ to work in factories.

B VOCABULARY

Complete each sentence with the correct word.

agile	exhibit	settlement
carpenter	fascinated	shawl
draped	graduated	

1. People enjoyed the photo

   _____ at the art gallery.

2. Ria wrapped herself in a

   _____ to keep warm.

3. When you are interested and delighted by

   something, you are _____ by that thing.

4. Before going out into the cold, Cheng-Yu

   _____ a scarf around his neck.

5. Dafna _____ from high school when she was eighteen years old.

6. People in the neighborhood took English

   classes at the _____ house.

7. The cat was so _____ that it could walk on a tightrope.

C · STORY REVIEW

Complete each sentence with *duckling, Toto, Buck, cat, Nellie,* or *Martha.*

1. _____ pulled a thousand-pound sled.

2. _____ used her nose to track somebody over a ridge.

3. _____ jumped over fences during a race.

4. The _____ discovered that he could fly.

5. The _____ made a bargain with a woman.

D · TIMELINES

Here are some events from the Jane Addams biography.

- A new factory law passes.
- Hull House opens.

Write the correct event after each date on the timeline.

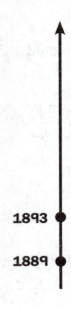

1893 ●

1889 ●

GO TO PART D IN YOUR TEXTBOOK

Name ______________________________

A STORY DETAILS

Work the items.

1. In what year did Rita Hansen become a resident of Hull House?

   ____

2. Jane Addams helped pass a law that prevented children under fourteen from working in ____________________.

3. Rita heard Jane tell a story about a boy who was ____________________ in a factory accident.

4. Jane said that boy should have been in ____________________ instead of working in a factory.

5. Hull House was located in Ward ____________________.

6. Jane said, "Hull House is a ____________________ bringing you and your neighbors together."

7. How did most of the residents at Hull House earn money?
   a. They had jobs downtown.
   b. They turned Hull House into a store.
   c. They charged immigrants for classes.

8. In 1893, women in the United States did not have the right to ____ .
   a. speak   b. vote   c. earn money

B VOCABULARY

Complete each sentence with the correct word.

draped	infant	shawl
exhibit	profit	supervisor
graduated	resident	ward

1. Abena ____________________ from high school when she was 18 years old.

2. Jingdan lived in the largest ____________________ in the city.

3. The ____________________ cried as soon as she was born.

4. The cashier couldn't take a break until his ____________________ said he could.

5. It cost ten dollars to see the ____________________ of paintings by Picasso.

6. The ice cream peddler made much more ____________________ in the summer than in the winter.

7. A ____________________ of New York is called a New Yorker.

Copyright © McGraw-Hill Education

C   STORY REVIEW

Work the items.

1. Jane Addams lived in the city of

   _____ .

2. The street one mile west of that city's downtown area is called

   _____ Street.

3. The house Jane Addams opened on that

   street is called _____ House.

4. The neighborhood around that house was ▢ .

   a. rich   b. poor   c. middle class

5. Which country did Maria's family come

   from? _____

D   TIMELINES

Here are some events.

• Hull House opens.

• A new factory law passes.

Write the correct event after each date on the timeline.

1893 ●

1889 ●

GO TO PART D IN YOUR TEXTBOOK

A STORY DETAILS

Work the items.

1. During the day, Rita worked at a

_____ , but at night she

worked at _____

_____ .

2. Rita felt her night job was more ▨▨▨ than
her day job.

   a. well-paying   b. time-consuming

   c. important

3. Rita made speeches to raise ▨▨▨ .

   a. money   b. rents   c. prices

4. The person who owned the worst
buildings in Ward 19 was named William

_____ .

5. At first, how did Rita's parents feel about
her job at Hull House?

   a. They admired it.

   b. They were upset.

   c. They were happy she had a job.

6. After Rita gave a speech at her parents'

house, Mr. _____
got angry.

7. That person owned a

_____ factory.

8. The character who worked for that person

was named _____

_____ .

B VOCABULARY

**Complete each sentence with the
correct word.**

criticized	infant	resident
filth	invest	supervisor
fined	profit	ward

1. Namid decided to _____
his money in a bicycle company.

2. The movie was bad, and many people

_____ it.

3. You can be _____ if you
park your car in a loading zone.

4. You have to be a _____
of a state to get a driver's license from
that state.

5. The empty lot smelled, and it was covered

with _____ .

6. It's hard to make a _____
if you don't have any customers.

7. The new mother took a photo of her

_____ sleeping.

C PERSPECTIVES

Complete each sentence with *important* **or** *unimportant.*

1. Rita Hansen thought that counting money at the bank was _____ .

2. Rita thought that changing twenty-dollar bills was _____ .

3. Rita thought that talking to poor people about their problems was

   _____ .

4. Rita thought that adding up numbers was

   _____ .

5. Rita thought that making speeches to raise money for Hull House was

   _____ .

6. Rita thought that teaching English classes was _____ .

D FACT OR FICTION

Write whether each statement is *fact* **or** *fiction.*

1. The Greeks believed that Zeus was the chief deity. _____

2. Zeus talked to people. _____

3. Jane Addams started Hull House.

   _____

4. The Beast changed into the prince.

   _____

E CHARACTER STATEMENTS

Complete each sentence with *Hades,* *Hermes, Poseidon, Ares, Aphrodite,* **or** *Zeus.*

1. _____ said, "I carry a strange staff."

2. _____ said, "I am the god of the sea."

3. _____ said, "I command the thunder and lightning."

4. _____ said, "I am the goddess of love and beauty."

5. _____ said, "I am the god of war."

F CLASSIFICATION

Write whether each animal is *wild* **or** *domestic.*

1. Lion _____

2. Monkey _____

3. Hound _____

4. Goat _____

5. Orangutan _____

6. Whale _____

7. Chicken _____

GO TO PART D IN YOUR TEXTBOOK

A STORY DETAILS

Work the items.

1. In what year did Camila Perez fly from New York to Chicago?

   _____

2. In what year did Jane Addams open Hull House? _____

3. By the time Camila flew to Chicago, Hull House had become a community with _____ buildings.

4. In the 1930s, the United States was in a _____ called the Great _____ .

5. Camila's plane trip from New York to Chicago took nearly ▓▓▓ hours.

   a. two   b. eight   c. twenty

6. Camila fell into ▓▓▓ when she thought about Jane Addams.

   a. a reverie   b. a deep sleep

   c. the seat in front of her

7. Why did Jane Addams travel to Europe in 1915?

   a. to help the United States win World War One

   b. to establish new settlement houses

   c. to try to stop World War One

8. In what year did Jane Addams return to Europe? _____

9. Jane Addams said, "All the people in the world are _____ ."

B VOCABULARY

Complete each sentence with the correct word.

abandon	filth	reverie
criticize	fined	
depression	invested	

1. The country was in a _____ , so it was hard to find a job.

2. You need to be careful when you _____ other people.

3. While watching the movie, Rance had a _____ about being a movie star.

4. The judge _____ Mariko two hundred dollars for running a red light.

5. The hikers had to _____ the idea of reaching the mountain top because the mountain was too steep.

6. The cook's friends _____ a lot of money in her new restaurant.

C ROMAN DEITIES

**Complete each sentence with *Jupiter,
Mars, Mercury, Neptune, Pluto,* or *Venus*.**

1. _____ had wings on
his sandals.

2. _____ ruled the ocean.

3. _____ commanded
the thunder.

4. _____ was in love with the
god of war.

5. _____ was the god of
the underworld.

D PICTURE CLUES

   A   B   C

Work the items.

1. Which picture shows a place that would
hold an animal's scent well?
   - A   • B   • C

2. Which picture shows a place that would
hold an animal's scent, but not too well?
   - A   • B   • C

3. Which picture shows a place that would
not hold an animal's scent?
   - A   • B   • C

GO TO PART D IN YOUR TEXTBOOK

A STORY DETAILS

Work the items.

1. Jane Addams received the

_____ Peace Prize.

2. In what year did Jane Addams receive that

prize? _____

3. Why did Jane Addams drop out of
medical school?

   a. She wanted to study another field.

   b. Her health was poor.

   c. She flunked her classes.

4. The person helping in the kitchen at Hull

House was _____

_____ .

5. The person who had retired from
her job as vice president of a

bank was _____

_____ .

6. In what year did Jane Addams die?

_____

7. Camila said that Jane Addams was not
really dead because she lived in
people's ▮▮▮ .

   a. minds   b. books   c. hearts

B VOCABULARY

Complete each sentence with the correct word.

abandon	interviews	spectacular
awarded	Nobel	
depression	reverie	

1. President Obama received the

_____ Peace Prize in 2009.

2. Every day Mika had the same

_____ about becoming
president of the world.

3. The sailors had to _____
their ship when it began to sink.

4. The snow-topped mountains were a

_____ sight.

5. The vegetable farmer was

_____ a blue ribbon at the
fair for her amazing green beans.

6. On many TV shows, the host

_____ different guests.

C STORY REVIEW

Complete each sentence with the correct word.

1. The first African American baseball player in the major leagues was Jackie

   _____ .

2. That player played for the Brooklyn

   _____ .

3. The home field for that team was

   _____ Field.

4. The general manager of that team was

   Branch _____ .

D TIMELINES

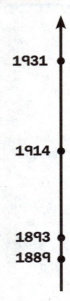

1931 ●

1914 ●

1893 ●
1889 ●

Here are some events:

- World War One begins.
- Hull House opens.
- Jane Addams wins the Nobel Peace Prize.
- A new factory law passes.

Write the correct event after each date on the timeline.

GO TO PART D IN YOUR TEXTBOOK

A STORY DETAILS

Work the items.

1. What's the title of the next novel you will read?

   _____

2. In which country does the novel take

   place? _____

3. About how many years ago does the novel take place?

   a. 50   b. 250   c. 500

4. Peddlers in London sold traps for

   catching _____ .

5. Which travelers went fastest on the roads?

   a. messengers   b. people in wagons

   c. people walking

6. Poor farmers had a famous saying that

   "Sheep _____

   _____ ."

7. What material did people use to build ships?

   a. polyester   b. plastic   c. wood

8. People used coal for building

   _____ .

9. What metal did workers produce in blast

   furnaces? _____

B VOCABULARY

Complete each sentence with the correct word.

awarded	inland	plumbing
furnace	interview	scurried
hardware	pauper	spectacular

1. Workers heaved the rocks into the blast

   _____ and waited for the

   iron in the rocks to melt.

2. The Tompkins' cabin had no indoor

   _____ , so they had to

   drink bottled water.

3. Olga went to the _____

   store to buy a hammer and nails.

4. The mouse _____ quickly

   along the kitchen wall and hid under

   the stove.

5. The rich man gambled away all his money

   and ended up a _____ .

6. The boat traveled twenty miles up the

   river before reaching an

   _____ port.

7. Pazi was _____ first place

   for spelling all the words correctly.

C MAPS

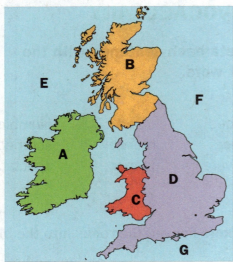

Work the items.

1. What is the name of country A?
   _____

2. What is the name of country B?
   _____

3. What is the name of country C?
   _____

4. What is the name of country D?
   _____

5. Which city does the dot show?
   _____

6. What body of water does E show?
   _____

7. What body of water does F show?
   _____

8. What body of water does G show?
   _____

D COMPARE AND CONTRAST

Complete each sentence with *2000s* or *1500s and 2000s*.

1. Houses in the
   _____
   had fireplaces.

2. Houses in the
   _____ had
   digital clocks.

3. Houses in the
   _____
   had mousetraps.

4. Houses in the
   _____ had
   cooking pots.

5. Houses in the
   _____ had
   gas heaters.

6. Houses in the
   _____
   had showers.

7. Houses in the
   _____ had
   loaves of bread.

8. Houses in the
   _____
   had computers.

GO TO PART E IN YOUR TEXTBOOK

A STORY DETAILS

Work the items.

1. Henry the _____ was the richest man in England in 1501.

2. The Prince of Wales is the

   _____ son of the king or queen of England.

3. Henry the _____ ruled England from 1509 to 1547.

4. This king believed that only ▮ were fit to rule England.

   a. women   b. men   c. duchesses

5. How many wives did this king have?

   _____

6. Complete the saying about this king's wives.

   Divorced, _____ ,

   _____ ;

   Divorced, _____ ,

   _____ .

7. The prince in *The Prince and the Pauper*

   became _____ the Sixth.

8. Queen Mary was called

   _____ Mary.

9. The last Tudor ruler was

   _____ the First.

B LORDS AND LADIES

The list shows lords and ladies in order of their power. Fill in the blanks to complete the list.

1. duke _____

2. _____ marchioness

3. earl _____

4. _____

   _____

5. _____

   _____

C TIMELINES

The timeline shows the years when each Tudor's rule began. Write the correct name next to each year.

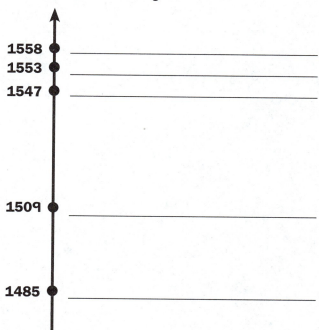

1558 ● _____

1553 ● _____

1547 ● _____

1509 ● _____

1485 ● _____

D CHARACTER TRAITS

Complete each sentence with *Edward the Sixth, Elizabeth the First, Henry the Seventh, Henry the Eighth,* or *Mary the First.*

1. _____ died at the age of sixteen.

2. _____ wanted a son more than anything else.

3. _____ was the last Tudor to rule England.

4. _____ was the first Tudor to rule England.

5. _____ had six wives.

GO TO PART C IN YOUR TEXTBOOK

A STORY DETAILS

Work the items.

1. The two main classes in England in the 1500s were _____ people and _____ people.

2. Some lords and ladies lived in big country houses called _____ .

3. The rooms in these houses were heated with ▊ .

   a. electricity   b. gas   c. wood

4. The master of these houses was called the _____ .

5. The person who ran these houses was called the _____ .

6. The main food that the master and his family ate was ▊ .

   a. meat   b. vegetables   c. bread

7. In the 1580s, an explorer brought a strange vegetable called a _____ from America to England.

8. Books became less expensive in the 1400s after a goldsmith in Germany invented the _____ press.

9. William Shakespeare became famous in the late 1500s by writing _____ for theaters.

B VOCABULARY

Complete each sentence with the correct word.

carve	opportunity	plumbing
hardware	pauper	scurry
inland	playwright	supervise

1. Shakespeare was best known as a _____ , but he also wrote poems.

2. It took a long time to _____ the designs in the table legs.

3. The teacher gave each student one _____ to answer the difficult question.

4. The _____ town was right in the middle of the country.

5. The school bus driver had to _____ the children to make sure they behaved.

6. Isra lost so much money playing the lottery that she became a _____ .

7. Jamal had to drive ten miles to the _____ store to buy ten nails.

D CLASSIFICATION

- The statements below describe people in England in the 1500s.

Complete each sentence with *Rich*, *Poor*, or *Rich and poor*.

1. _____ people ate mainly meat.

2. _____ people watched plays.

3. _____ people followed orders in the kitchen.

4. _____ people lived in manors.

5. _____ people slept in beds with posts at all four corners.

C MAPS

Work the items.

1. Country **A** is named

   _____ .

2. Country **B** is named

   _____ .

3. Country **C** is named

   _____ .

4. Country **D** is named

   _____ .

5. The dot in country **D** shows a city

   named _____ .

E CHARACTER TRAITS

- The statements below describe people in England in the 1500s.

Complete each sentence with *rich* or *poor*.

1. Lords and ladies were

   _____ .

2. Coal miners were _____ .

3. Peddlers were _____ .

4. The Royal Family was

   _____ .

5. Except for sheep farmers, most farmers

   were _____ .

GO TO PART D IN YOUR TEXTBOOK

A STORY DETAILS

Work the items.

1. During the 1500s, many English peasants lost their land to rich

   _____ farmers.

2. Queen Elizabeth helped the peasants by asking rich farmers to ▮ .

   a. raise the peasants' wages

   b. grow rice

   c. stop raising so many sheep

3. The floor in a peasant's hut was usually

   made of _____ , and the

   roof was made of _____ .

4. There was usually a _____
   in the middle of a peasant's hut.

5. Which of these items were **not** found in peasants' huts?

   a. beds   b. stools   c. tables

   d. chairs   e. benches

6. Poor people's clothes were made of cotton or ▮ .

   a. wool   b. silk   c. velvet

7. Which of these items were peasants forbidden to wear?

   a. shirts   b. jewels   c. dresses

   d. pants   e. socks

B VOCABULARY

Complete each sentence with the correct word.

brand	firstborn	outlive
childbirth	forbidden	peasant
confine	optimistic	stocks

1. The lord lived in a manor, but the

   _____ lived in a hut.

2. The judge decided to _____
   the criminal in a large prison.

3. The rancher used a hot iron to

   _____ her cows.

4. The jailer put the prisoner's feet

   into the _____ .

5. The Prince of Wales is the

   _____ son of an English
   king or queen.

6. The happy coach felt _____
   that her team would win the soccer game.

7. The dog was _____ to
   sleep on the couch.

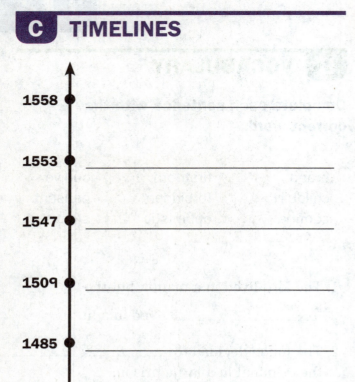

1558 • _____

1553 • _____

1547 • _____

1509 • _____

1485 • _____

Write the name of each Tudor ruler next to the year their rule began.

• The statements below describe people in England in the 1500s.

Complete each sentence with *Rich, Poor,* or *Rich and poor.*

1. _____ people lived in one-room huts.

2. _____ people used fireplaces to stay warm.

3. _____ people wore clothes that were made of velvet.

4. _____ people wore jewels in their hats.

5. _____ people could be punished for wearing socks.

6. _____ people enjoyed watching plays.

GO TO PART D IN YOUR TEXTBOOK

A STORY DETAILS

Work the items.

1. A fathom is _____ feet long.

2. When water is at "mark twain," it is _____ feet deep.

3. Sam Clemens grew up in the town of _____ , Missouri.

4. Sam's first job was with a ▨▨▨ .

   a. steamboat   b. book publisher

   c. newspaper

5. Sam used the name Mark Twain to sign his ▨▨ articles.

   a. serious   b. humorous

   c. longest

6. Twain's most famous story is about a jumping _____ .

7. One of the books Twain wrote in Hartford is called *Huckleberry* _____ .

8. Twain went bankrupt by investing in a ▨▨ .

   a. printing press   b. steamboat

   c. stock market

9. *The Prince and the Pauper* takes place during the ▨▨ .

   a. 1500s   b. 1600s   c. 1800s

B VOCABULARY

Complete each sentence with the correct word.

bankrupt	fathoms	lecture
confined	forbidden	optimistic
craft	humorous	

1. The lake was five _____ deep.

2. People laughed at the _____ movie.

3. The professor gave a _____ on monkeys.

4. In the zoo, the lion was _____ to a cage.

5. A canoe is a common type of water _____ .

6. The woman became _____ when her restaurant failed.

7. The coach was _____ that her team would win.

C TIMELINES

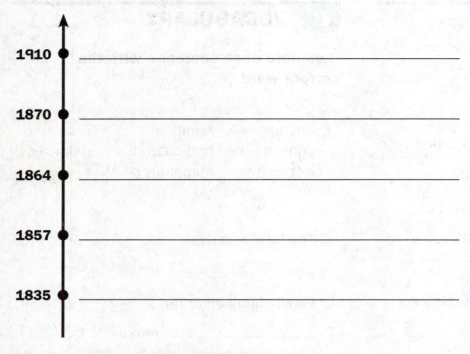

1910 _____

1870 _____

1864 _____

1857 _____

1835 _____

Write the correct event after each date on the timeline.

- Mark Twain dies in Connecticut.
- Mark Twain is born in Missouri.
- Mark Twain marries Olivia Langdon.
- Mark Twain publishes "The Jumping Frog."
- Mark Twain learns how to pilot a steamboat.

GO TO PART D IN YOUR TEXTBOOK

A STORY DETAILS

Work the items.

1. In what year were Tom Canty and Edward Tudor born? _____

2. They were born in ▢ .

   a. England   b. Scotland

   c. Wales

3. Tom earned money for his family by ▢ .

   a. begging   b. princely behavior

   c. stealing

4. How many rooms did Tom's family live in? _____

5. Tom dreamed of becoming a _____ .

6. After Tom learned to read, his friends treated him with ▢ .

   a. contempt   b. respect

   c. medicine

7. One day, Tom walked to _____ Palace.

8. A family named _____ lived in that palace.

9. Tom pressed his face against the palace gate to ▢ the prince.

   a. beg from   b. wave to

   c. look at

B VOCABULARY

Complete each sentence with the correct word.

bankrupt	fathom	manners
craft	gifted	regard
enchanted	ignorant	unleash

1. People who entered the _____ castle became the wizard's prisoners.

2. After the wheel broke, the cowgirl had to _____ the horses from the wagon.

3. The kindergarten student was so _____ about numbers that he couldn't add two and two.

4. Some people _____ the general as a hero, but others think she's a coward.

5. Parents teach their children _____ so the children know how to behave in public.

6. The _____ musician could play the guitar perfectly when he was only four years old.

7. An aircraft carrier is a giant _____ .

Complete each sentence with *John Canty*, *Tom Canty*, or *Edward Tudor*.

1. _____ was
   born into a family that did not want him.

2. _____ was
   dressed in silk clothes.

3. _____
   pretended to be a prince.

4. _____ had a
   family that was happy when he was born.

5. _____ was
   a thief.

6. _____ had to
   beg for money.

Number the events in the correct sequence.

____ Jane Addams wins the Nobel Prize.

____ A new factory law passes.

____ World War One begins.

____ Hull House opens.

GO TO PART F IN YOUR TEXTBOOK

A   STORY DETAILS

Work the items.

1. At the beginning of the chapter, Edward told the guard to open the

   _____ for Tom.

2. Who did Edward think should help Tom's sisters get dressed?

   a. Tom's mother

   b. Tom's grandmother

   c. servants

3. When Edward and Tom talked about entertainment, Tom's answers made Edward feel ▨ .

   a. angry   b. envious

   c. distressed

4. After Edward and Tom talked about their lives, they decided to

   _____ places.

5. When Edward and Tom stood in front of the mirror, they discovered that they

   looked _____ the same except for one difference.

6. The one difference was that Tom had a ▨ on his hand.

   a. wart   b. ring   c. bruise

7. Edward went back to the gate to ▨ the guard who had shoved Tom.

   a. punish   b. reward   c. ignore

8. At the end of the chapter, nobody in the crowd believed that Edward was the

   Prince of _____ .

B   VOCABULARY

Complete each sentence with the correct word.

gesture	lecture	rudely
humorous	outfit	salute
hustled	peasant	tattered

1. The rich lady wore a different

   _____ every day.

2. The soldiers raised their hands to their

   foreheads to _____ the general.

3. The firefighters _____ people out of the burning building.

4. Alfonso acted so _____ at the party that the host asked him to leave.

5. The beggar's coat was so

   _____ that it looked like Swiss cheese.

6. The standard _____ for asking someone to speak louder is to put your hands behind your ears.

7. Hamza thought his joke was funny, but his mother didn't think it was

   _____ at all.

C CHARACTER TRAITS

Complete each sentence with *Tom Canty,
Edward Tudor,* or *John Canty.*

1. _____ played
   tag in the river.

2. _____ spent
   most of his time inside.

3. _____ liked
   to pretend that he was somebody else.

4. _____ could
   not play with other boys.

5. People helped
   _____ do
   almost everything.

D REFERRING TO TEXT

In the following passage, underline the
sentence that shows why Edward wanted
to be like Tom.

"Tell me, what do you do for entertainment?"
Edward asked.

Tom explained the races, games, swimming,
and other things he did for fun. "We have the
most fun in the river," Tom observed. "We play
tag and dunk each other in the water."

Edward leaned back and looked up at the
ceiling. "Oh," he said slowly, "I wish I could have
such pleasant experiences."

Tom continued. He told Edward about the
neighborhood dances, about making mud pies,
and about being buried in the sand.

GO TO PART D IN YOUR TEXTBOOK

A STORY DETAILS

Work the items.

1. After Edward became ▮▮▮ , the crowd stopped tormenting him.

   a. dignified   b. silent   c. angry

2. The paving stones hurt the ▮▮▮ of Edward's bare feet.

   a. soles   b. souls   c. shoals

3. Edward suddenly knew where he was when he approached ▮▮▮ .

   a. Westminster Palace

   b. a large church

   c. Tom's house

4. The schoolboys Edward met looked like someone had put a _____ over their heads before cutting their hair.

5. When Edward got angry at the schoolboys, he tried to reach for the _____ at his hip, but it wasn't there.

6. Edward remembered that Tom lived on _____ Lane.

7. John Canty believed that Edward was ▮▮▮ .

   a. Edward Tudor

   b. the Prince of Wales

   c. Tom Canty

8. John Canty told Edward, "Be glad you're not getting the _____ of your life."

B VOCABULARY

Complete each sentence with the correct word.

alley	gifted	saucer
dignity	hive	soles
enchanted	ignorant	torment

1. The hiker walked so much that she wore out the _____ of her shoes.

2. The restaurant kitchen was a _____ of activity.

3. In some cities, people put their garbage cans in the _____ behind their houses.

4. The cat began to _____ the mouse with its sharp claws.

5. No matter what happened in her courtroom, the judge always acted with _____ .

6. The coffee overflowed from the cup into the _____ .

7. Birds could talk and deer could sing in the _____ forest.

C | PLACE NAMES

Complete each sentence with
Connecticut, London, Mississippi, Missouri,
Pudding, or *Westminster.*

1. Mark Twain grew up in Hannibal,

   _____ .

2. Edward Tudor lived in

   _____ Palace.

3. Mark Twain piloted a steamboat on the

   _____ River.

4. Tom Canty lived on

   _____ Lane.

5. Both Edward and Tom lived in the city of

   _____ , England.

GO TO PART D IN YOUR TEXTBOOK

A STORY DETAILS

Work the items.

1. At the beginning of the chapter, Tom spent time _____ as a prince in front of a mirror.

2. The girl who entered the prince's apartment was Lady Jane _____ .

3. As Tom spoke to that girl, he ▢ .
   a. stood straight
   b. ordered her to bow
   c. bowed to her

4. The girl believed that the prince had gone ▢ .
   a. mad   b. fishing   c. away

5. The king's name was _____ the _____ .

6. The king thought that Tom was his _____ .

7. Tom gave the correct answer to the king's question about _____ .

8. Tom couldn't answer when the king gave him a question in _____ .

9. The king thought the prince had become mad from too much ▢ .
   a. playing   b. sleeping
   c. reading

B VOCABULARY

Complete each sentence with the correct word.

gesture	outfit	regain
hustle	patrician	stricken
merciful	posing	

1. Because the man was a lord, he was a _____ .

2. The police officer made a _____ with her hand to stop traffic.

3. Rance was panic- _____ when he saw the spider crawling up his arm.

4. The prisoner begged the judge to be _____ .

5. It takes a while to _____ your senses after you faint.

6. The actor used a mirror to practice _____ as a character in a play.

7. For his tennis _____ , Omar always wore tennis shoes, short pants, a T-shirt, and a baseball hat.

C PERSPECTIVES

Complete each sentence with *crazy* or *normal*.

1. The king thought it was

   _____ for Edward to wear silk clothes.

2. The king thought it was

   _____ for Edward to call him "Father."

3. The king thought it was

   _____ for Edward to ask about going to Pudding Lane.

4. The king thought it was

   _____ for Edward to bow down to Lady Jane Grey.

5. The king thought it was

   _____ for Edward to know about history.

6. The king thought it was

   _____ for Edward not to speak French.

D WORD ENDINGS

Each item shows a root word and a word ending. Write the combined word.

1. uneasy / ness _____

2. mercy / ful _____

3. magnificent / ence _____

4. activity / ies _____

5. pose / ing _____

6. misery / able _____

GO TO PART D IN YOUR TEXTBOOK

A STORY DETAILS

Work the items.

1. Tom's teacher was called the Earl of

   _____ .

2. Tom was supposed to attend the Lord

   Mayor's _____ in
   the evening.

3. Two girls came to visit Tom. Which one
   was his sister?

   _____

4. What was the other girl's name?

   _____

5. After the earl left Tom's apartment, he

   spoke to Lord _____

   _____ .

6. The earl believed that the king would

   soon _____ .

7. The name of the boy who was supposed
   to become king after Henry

   was _____ Tudor.

8. At the end of the chapter, the teacher
   concluded that the prince was ▉▉▉ .

   a. crazy   b. an identical boy

   c. faking illness

9. Before that, the teacher thought the prince
   might be ▉▉▉ .

   a. crazy   b. an identical boy

   c. faking illness

B VOCABULARY

**Complete each sentence with the
correct word.**

banquet	madman	salute
dismissed	page	subject
identical	rudely	tattered

1. The weather is one _____
   that everybody can talk about.

2. The teacher _____ the
   class for lunch exactly at noon.

3. The pauper wore _____
   clothes that hadn't been washed
   in months.

4. Everybody at the _____
   commented on how good the food was.

5. The real diamond and the fake diamond

   looked _____ to everybody
   except the expert.

6. The lord commanded his

   _____ to bring the lord's
   horse to the gate.

7. The soldiers believed their general was

   a _____ who
   acted recklessly.

C STORY REVIEW

Complete each sentence.

1. If there's not a tie, a baseball game lasts for _____ innings.

2. When a baseball team is not batting, it has _____ players on the field.

3. To score a run, a baseball player must cross _____ plate.

4. In a baseball game, the _____ calls the balls and strikes.

5. The baseball player who plays between the second baseman and the third baseman is called the _____ .

6. The baseball player who throws balls and strikes is called the _____ .

D PERSPECTIVES

Complete each sentence with *crazy* or *normal*.

1. People thought it was _____ for the prince to pour his own glass of water.

2. People thought it was _____ for the prince to call Princess Elizabeth his sister.

3. People thought it was _____ for the prince to say that his father was a thief.

4. People thought it was _____ for the prince to make his servants go away with gestures.

5. People thought it was _____ for the prince to speak French.

GO TO PART E IN YOUR TEXTBOOK

A STORY DETAILS

Work the items.

1. The Lord Chief _____
   fastened a napkin around Tom's neck.

2. The Taster to his Highness had a
   dangerous job because he could be ▓ .
   a. poisoned   b. overfed
   c. cooked

3. About how many servants did Tom
   have altogether?
   a. 40   b. 200   c. 400

4. When the servants saw Tom's behavior,
   they were moved to ▓ .
   a. laughter   b. pity   c. respect

5. Tom ask the servant to take his napkin
   away because he was afraid it would get
   _____ .

6. When Tom's nose began to itch, he asked
   the servants, "What is the
   _____ for this emergency?"

7. At the end of the meal, Tom drank
   _____ water.

8. Pieces from a suit of _____
   were hanging on a wall in
   Tom's apartment.

9. The book Tom read told how to
   _____ in the English court.

Copyright © McGraw-Hill Education

B VOCABULARY

Complete each sentence with the correct word.

banquet	diaper	inspected
butler	dismiss	pestering
custom	identical	rose

1. In the castle, the _____
   told the other servants what to do.

2. The napkin was made of soft
   _____ .

3. The police officer _____
   the crime scene for evidence.

4. The princess waved her hand to
   _____ her servants.

5. The dinner guests used
   _____ water to clean
   their fingers.

6. The people who lived on the island had a
   strange _____ of only
   sleeping in boats.

7. The horse shook its mane because the
   flies kept _____ it.

C ROYAL SERVANTS

Complete each sentence with *Butler*, *Diaperer*, *Scratcher*, or *Water Pourer*.

1. The Lord Chief

   _____ was in

   charge of the other servants.

2. The Lord Chief

   _____ was in

   charge of the napkins.

3. The Lord Chief

   _____ didn't

   exist, but he would have been in charge of

   the prince's nose.

4. The Lord Chief

   _____ stood

   behind Tom's chair to oversee the meal.

5. The Lord Chief

   _____ held

   a pitcher.

GO TO PART D IN YOUR TEXTBOOK

A STORY DETAILS

Work the items.

1. At the beginning of the chapter, Edward was trapped in a room rented by the _____ .

2. At the beginning of the chapter, Tom was in _____ Palace.

3. Tom's mother thought that Tom's foolish ▮▮ had ruined his mind.

   a. writing   b. reading   c. games

4. Canty took Edward with him to get money for ▮▮ .

   a. food   b. rent   c. blankets

5. The large man said that Canty _____ him money.

6. Canty told Edward to go to the far end of _____ Bridge if they got separated.

7. As soon as Canty let go of him, Edward ▮▮ .

   a. returned to the palace

   b. went to London Bridge

   c. ran off

8. That evening was the Lord Mayor's _____ .

9. That event was to be held at _____ .

B VOCABULARY

Complete each sentence with the correct word.

advantage	page	subject
custom	retreat	toils
lumbered	stout	

1. The fox was stuck in the _____ , but it gnawed its way to freedom.

2. The huge football player _____ through the crowd like an ox.

3. Even though he was weak, Shim didn't let anybody take _____ of him.

4. The battle was lost, so the army decided to _____ .

5. Not even the fierce wind could sway the _____ tree.

6. The fans talked about many things, but the main _____ was sports.

C CHARACTER TRAITS

Complete each sentence with *Only Edward* or *Both Tom and Edward*.

1. _____ could read a book.

2. _____ knew how to speak French.

3. _____ would expect someone to dress him in the morning.

4. _____ could wear the clothes of the Prince of Wales.

5. _____ was the brother of Princess Elizabeth.

D WORD ENDINGS

The box contains root words and endings. Complete each sentence with a root word plus an ending.

elect	ion
infect	ive
inspect	or

1. A person who examines crimes closely is called an _____ .

2. An event where people vote is called an _____ .

3. When you see a doctor, he or she gives you a complete _____ .

4. When something can spread a disease, it is _____ .

5. People vote on candidates for _____ offices.

6. When a cut in your finger gets red and swollen, you have an _____ .

GO TO PART D IN YOUR TEXTBOOK

A STORY DETAILS

Work the items.

1. The barges traveled on the River

   _____ .

2. Two pages held white

   _____ as they walked in
   front of the lords and ladies.

3. The name of the Lord Mayor of London's

   banquet hall was _____ .

4. What did the people do when Tom
   stood up?

   a. stood up

   b. said, "Long live the King."

   c. cheered

5. What did Tom do to signal the start of
   the banquet?

   a. told people to begin eating

   b. stood up

   c. drank from a golden cup

6. The person who helped Edward

   was named _____

   _____ .

7. The horsemen shouted, "Make way for

   the king's _____ !"

8. What news did that person bring to
   the banquet?

   a. Long live the king.

   b. The king is dead.

   c. The prince has gone mad.

B VOCABULARY

**Complete each sentence with the
correct word.**

barge	lumber	toils
file	retreat	vast
lantern	stout	wand

1. The sailors gazed at the

   _____ ocean on all sides
   of them.

2. A long _____ of ants
   marched from the anthill to the
   picnic table.

3. Dozens of people sat in the

   _____ as it slowly moved
   up the river.

4. When people saw the servant with a

   _____ , they knew the
   queen would soon appear.

5. The only light in the campground came

   from a battered old _____ .

6. The bulldog was small, but she was as

   _____ as a fire hydrant.

7. When it began to rain, we decided

   to _____ indoors.

C   SEQUENCING

Number the events in the correct sequence.

_____ Tom became King of England.

_____ Tom stepped onto the royal barge.

_____ Miles stepped forward to help Edward.

_____ A messenger entered the banquet.

_____ Miles and Edward ran from the crowd.

D   CHARACTER REVIEW

Complete each sentence with *Edward, Elizabeth, Hertford, Jane, John,* or *Tom.*

1. Edward's sister was named

   _____ Tudor.

2. The real Prince of Wales was named

   _____ .

3. The story said that _____ was the Prince of Poverty.

4. The prince's teacher was the Earl of

   _____ .

5. Edward's cousin was named

   Lady _____ Grey.

GO TO PART D IN YOUR TEXTBOOK

A STORY DETAILS

Work the items.

1. Miles was staying in an

   _____ .

2. Who was waiting for Edward on London Bridge?

   a. John Canty

   b. Tom Canty

   c. Miles Hendon

3. Miles's brother, _____ , had convinced their father to throw Miles out of the family castle.

4. Miles had been serving as a soldier in

   _____ for the last seven years.

5. Before Edward ate, he said that Miles could not _____ in the presence of the king.

6. Edward used a sword to make Miles a ▮▮▮ .

   a. soldier   b. knight   c. page

7. Unlike other lords, Miles could

   _____ in the presence of the king.

8. Miles believed that he was a knight in the

   kingdom of _____ .

B VOCABULARY

Complete each sentence with the correct word.

advantage	inn	regretted
blurred	madman	shudder
convince	page	subject

1. It's difficult to _____ somebody that they're wrong.

2. The loud scream made Hatsu

   _____ with fear.

3. Sunee _____ her rudeness toward her younger brother.

4. The photos Aman took from the moving

   car were _____ .

5. Ethan was so angry that he began to act

   like a _____ .

6. The weary travelers stayed at a cozy

   _____ next to the beach.

7. The people in the book club discussed

   only one _____ : books.

C POINT OF VIEW

For each sentence, write whether the point of view is *first-person*, *second-person*, or *third-person*.

1. You are surprised by the loud noise.

   _____

2. The quick red fox jumps over the lazy brown dog.

   _____

3. Those mean girls don't bother me.

   _____

4. I've never been to London.

   _____

5. Yukio played the guitar with great skill.

   _____

6. We cheered when our team won the game.

   _____

7. They were sad because their team lost the game.

   _____

8. You need to clean up your room or you can't go out to play.

   _____

GO TO PART D IN YOUR TEXTBOOK

A   STORY DETAILS

Work the items.

1. Where did Edward tell Miles to sleep?

   a. next to the bed

   b. in front of the door

   c. behind the door

2. Miles left the room to buy Edward some new _____ .

3. When Miles returned, he thought that _____ was still sleeping under the bed covers.

4. What was really under the bed covers?

   a. blankets and pillows

   b. Edward

   c. the innkeeper

5. The innkeeper told Miles that a _____ boy had come into the room.

6. That boy said that ▮▮ had sent him.

   a. John Canty   b. Miles Hendon

   c. Edward Tudor

7. The person who stepped from the crowd to follow Edward looked like a ▮▮ .

   a. messenger   b. nobleman

   c. ruffian

8. What did Miles resolve to do at the end of the chapter?

   a. forget about Edward

   b. find Edward

   c. return to the inn

B   VOCABULARY

Complete each sentence with the correct word.

barge	lantern	vast
disappearance	ruffian	wand
file	suspicious	

1. Something that is very large is _____ .

2. The crowd was puzzled by the _____ of the rabbit into the magician's hat.

3. People were _____ of the man who offered free money.

4. The sailors hung a _____ on the front of the boat so they could see in the dark.

5. The police chased after the _____ who had stolen the woman's purse.

6. Workers loaded the logs onto a _____ that floated down the river.

Copyright © McGraw-Hill Education

C POINT OF VIEW

For each sentence, write whether the point of view is *first-person*, *second-person*, or *third-person*.

1. The girls argued about who should sit in the front seat.
   _____

2. We met my uncle and the others in Chicago.
   _____

3. Why didn't I remember what I promised I would do?
   _____

4. You can visit your friends after you finish your homework.
   _____

5. The brown dog ran quickly after the tennis ball.
   _____

6. Could you please put your books over on that table?
   _____

7. I enjoyed watching the cats play with the ball of string.
   _____

D SEQUENCING

Number the events in the correct sequence.

_____ A messenger came to see Edward.

_____ Edward went to sleep.

_____ Miles left the inn to find clothes for Edward.

_____ Miles left the inn to find Edward.

_____ Miles talked to the innkeeper.

GO TO PART D IN YOUR TEXTBOOK

A STORY DETAILS

Work the items.

1. In his dream, Tom found a dozen

   _____ .

2. What did Tom decide to do with those
   objects in his dream?

   a. spend them as soon as possible

   b. keep them for himself

   c. give them to his mother

3. The dream showed that Tom wanted to
   ▊ .

   a. be king

   b. go home

   c. help Edward

4. One of Tom's socks was sent back because
   it had a _____ .

5. Tom conducted state business in the

   _____ room.

6. Hertford showed Tom when to stop
   talking by _____ in Tom's
   ear and _____ his head.

7. The whipping boy was named

   _____ .

8. Tom needed a whipping boy because Tom
   could not be _____ .

B VOCABULARY

**Complete each sentence with the
correct word.**

articles	garment	regret
assist	mourn	shatter
convince	ordeal	shudder

1. When you make somebody believe

   something, you _____ the
   person that what you're saying is true.

2. Another word for *shiver* is

   _____ .

3. Pants and shirts are _____
   of clothing.

4. Dishes made of clay and glass often

   _____ when you drop them
   on the floor.

5. Climbing up the mountain was a big

   _____ , but the view from
   the top was worth it.

6. A silk shirt is an expensive

   _____ .

7. The children gathered at the church to

   _____ their dead mother.

C   CHARACTER STATEMENTS

Below are statements that Henry the Eighth or Tom would probably make as king. Complete each sentence with _Henry_ or _Tom_.

1. _____ would probably say, "I will punish anybody who speaks against me."

2. _____ would probably say, "We have to start saving money."

3. _____ would probably say, "I want to wear the finest clothes."

4. _____ would probably say, "I will treat my subjects fairly."

5. _____ would probably say, "I want as much power as I can get."

D   POINT OF VIEW

For each sentence, write whether the point of view is _first-person_, _second-person_, or _third-person_.

1. We couldn't believe he did it.

   _____

2. She said that I was not her friend any more.

   _____

3. You are feeling sleepy, very sleepy.

   _____

4. The tree fell over without a sound.

   _____

5. Other than myself, nobody is paying attention.

   _____

6. All eyes were on the streaking rocket.

   _____

7. I told him that you are my best friend.

   _____

GO TO PART D IN YOUR TEXTBOOK

A STORY DETAILS

Work the items.

1. The king used the royal

   _____ to make

   papers official.

2. The sheriff said the accused man had ▨▨ another man.

   a. poisoned

   b. stabbed

   c. insulted

3. On New Year's Day, the accused man had jumped into the Thames and saved a

   boy from _____ .

4. The woman was accused of causing

   a powerful _____ .

5. The sheriff said the woman had caused that event by taking off her

   _____ .

6. When Edward ordered the woman to take off that article of clothing,

   _____ happened.

7. English law said that children could not

   make legal _____ .

8. One person in the throne room said, "The new king is as wise as he is ▨▨ ."

   a. intelligent

   b. crazy

   c. merciful

B VOCABULARY

Complete each sentence with the correct word.

conduct	inn	ruffian
disappearance	misplaced	seal
evidence	official	suspicious

1. When you don't trust someone, you are

   _____ of that person.

2. A rude and rough person is a

   _____ .

3. When you lead a meeting, you

   _____ the meeting.

4. A document that comes from a government office is an

   _____ document.

5. If you don't remember where you put

   something, you have _____ that thing.

6. Facts that help you conclude

   something are _____ .

7. A tool that puts a special mark on a piece

   of paper is called a _____ .

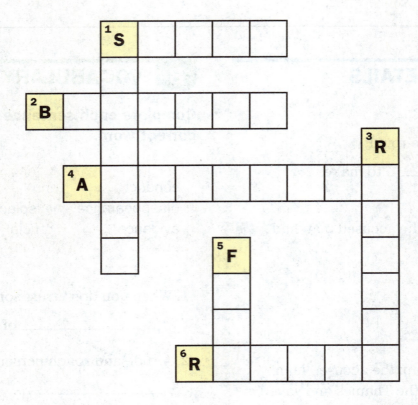

C CROSSWORD PUZZLE

Use CAPITAL LETTERS to complete the puzzle.

ACROSS

1. Something that is thick and sturdy is ▮▮▮ .

2. Things that do not look clear are ▮▮▮ .

4. When you treat someone unfairly for your own benefit, you take ▮▮▮ of that person.

6. When you are sorry about something that happened, you ▮▮▮ that thing.

DOWN

1. ▮▮▮ is another word for *shiver*.

3. When you move backward, you ▮▮▮ .

5. A line of people is called a ▮▮▮ of people.

GO TO PART D IN YOUR TEXTBOOK

A STORY DETAILS

Work the items.

1. Miles thought that Edward might go to
   _____ Hall if he escaped.

2. At the beginning of the chapter, it
   was hard to recognize John Canty
   because he ▓▓▓▓ .

   a. had lost a lot of weight

   b. was wearing a disguise

   c. had cut his hair

3. The messenger boy told Edward that Miles
   was lying _____ in
   the woods.

4. The messenger boy led Edward into a
   _____ next to a
   charred farmhouse.

5. John Canty's new last name was
   _____ .

6. Edward's new first name was
   _____ .

7. The messenger boy's first name was
   _____ .

8. Edward said, "I've fallen into a den of
   _____ ."

B VOCABULARY

**Complete each sentence with the
correct word.**

assist	expression	ordeal
charred	garment	sling
crutches	mourn	worming

1. When you help somebody, you
   _____ that person.

2. An extremely difficult experience is an
   _____ .

3. Lan put her broken arm into a
   _____ .

4. The second floor burned completely, but
   the first floor was only
   _____ .

5. The prisoner tried _____
   his way under the fence, but the guard
   saw everything.

6. After Haru broke his leg, he needed
   _____ to get around.

7. You could tell by the _____
   on Imena's face that she had lost the race.

C | CHARACTER DETAILS

Complete each sentence with *Canty*, *Edward*, *Hugo*, or *Miles*.

1. _____ had a new last name.

2. _____ had been tricked into following a boy.

3. _____ had delivered a fake message.

4. _____ decided to travel to Hendon Hall.

5. _____ thought his son was crazy.

D | SEQUENCING

Number the events in the correct sequence.

_____ Edward stayed in a barn.

_____ Edward let Tom into the palace.

_____ Edward stayed at an inn.

_____ Edward was thrown out of the palace.

E | POINT OF VIEW

Write whether each passage has *first-person*, *second-person*, or *third-person* point of view.

A. "I don't care what you do," said Michaela. "I'm staying here no matter what."

"I can't believe that," answered Zena. "This is going to be such a fun party."

The two girls glared at each other. Finally, Zena left. She couldn't figure out why Michaela didn't want to go to the party.

1. What is the point of view for passage A?

_____

B. The bicycle zoomed down the hill. It was going at least thirty miles an hour. Up ahead was a red traffic light. I squeezed on the brakes as hard as I could, but I couldn't slow down fast enough. Fortunately the light turned green just before the bicycle reached the intersection. I zoomed right through and finally stopped a block later.

2. What is the point of view for passage B?

_____

C. The weather is perfect, and there's not a cloud in the sky. The birds are already singing. You quickly put on your clothes and your hiking boots. Then you put on your backpack and head out the door. The state park is only fifteen minutes away. You look forward to exploring all the trails.

3. What is the point of view for passage C?

_____

GO TO PART D IN YOUR TEXTBOOK

A STORY DETAILS

Write the answers.

1. The "blind" man took the patches off his eyes so he could ▓▓▓ .

    a. rub his eyes   b. see

    c. clean the patches

2. The leader of the gang was the

    _____ .

3. The first time people were caught begging they were _____ .

4. The second time people were caught begging, they were _____ on the cheek and sold as

    _____ .

5. If beggars tried to run away, they were hunted down and ▓▓▓ .

    a. imprisoned   b. chained

    c. hanged

6. The man who had been punished for begging was _____ Burns.

7. The gang started calling Edward

    _____ the First, King of the

    _____ .

8. Edward was enthroned on a

    _____ .

B VOCABULARY

Complete each sentence with the correct word.

brawl	lash	prosper
burly	limb	vagrant
chant	mooncalf	

1. The _____ refused to wear a raincoat during the storm, so she got soaking wet and came down with a cold.

2. The bank door was protected by a _____ guard who could barely fit into his uniform.

3. It's difficult to _____ when you don't have a well-paying job.

4. The crowd began to _____ so loudly that the players used earplugs.

5. The arm is a _____ , but the nose isn't.

6. The _____ wandered from town to town, looking for work.

7. Many people were hurt during the violent _____ .

C POINT OF VIEW

Write whether each passage has *first-person*, *second-person*, or *third-person* point of view.

A. Climbing to the top of the mountain is hard. The path starts out with a gentle slope, but it gets steeper in a hurry. And then there's the poison oak. If you take just one step off the path, you brush against these evil plants, and you might get a bad rash. It's hard to get all the way to the top while staying on the path.

1. What is the point of view for passage A?

_____

B. "Do you think the test will be very hard?" asked Omar.

"I don't think so," answered Ida. "We've already practiced the words many times."

"Yes, but she might add some new words that we don't know," he said.

"I doubt that," she answered.

I wondered which person was right.

2. What is the point of view for passage B?

_____

C. The sun was blazing hot, and the sand on the beach was even hotter. People had put up big umbrellas so they could sit in the shade. Some people didn't care and just sat in the sun. Other people, mostly kids, splashed in the ocean and body surfed. One of them ran up to me and asked if I wanted to go swimming.

3. What is the point of view for passage C?

_____

GO TO PART E IN YOUR TEXTBOOK

Name _____

A STORY DETAILS

Work the items.

1. In the morning, what kind of mood were some of the vagrants in?

   a. joyous   b. content   c. irritable

2. The Ruffler ordered _____ not to be too rough with Edward.

3. How did the gang greet strangers along the road?

   a. insulted them

   b. begged for money

   c. ignored them

4. The gang had breakfast at a _____ house.

5. The gang threatened to _____ the house if they were reported.

6. When the friendly man approached Hugo and Edward, Hugo ⬛ on the ground.

   a. squirmed   b. danced   c. spat

7. The coin that Hugo asked for was a _____ .

8. Edward said the friendly man could make a _____ by hitting Hugo with his staff.

B VOCABULARY

Complete each sentence with the correct word.

charred	expression	motley
clothesline	eye	risk
crutches	irritable	sling

1. Pedro hung his wet garments on a _____ to dry.

2. Winona did not want to run the _____ of getting wet, so she brought an umbrella.

3. Isabel was so _____ that nobody dared to talk to her.

4. The dog had a _____ collection of chew toys and stuffed animals.

5. The cat began to _____ the mouse hole with hungry interest.

6. The pitcher had to keep her pitching arm in a _____ between innings.

7. You could tell by the _____ on their faces that the team had lost the game.

Copyright © McGraw-Hill Education

C | STORY REVIEW

Each statement describes a character in a story. For each statement, write the title of the story.

- The Cat that Walked by Himself
- The Miraculous Pitcher
- The Ugly Duckling
- Beauty and the Beast
- For the Love of a Man
- The Golden Touch
- A Horse to Remember
- Adventure on the Rocky Ridge

1. A girl who rode in horse races

_____

2. A girl who asked for a rose

_____

3. A man who had an insane love for gold

_____

4. An animal who turned into a swan

_____

5. An animal who made a good bargain

_____

6. An animal who pulled a heavy sled

_____

7. An old couple who were kind to strangers

_____

D | RELATED FACTS

Write the answers.

1. How many innings does a baseball game last unless it ends in a tie?

_____

2. When a team is not batting, how many of its players are on the field?

_____

3. How many teams bat during an inning?

_____

4. The player behind home plate is the

_____ .

5. The player who throws balls and strikes is the _____ .

6. The player who plays between the third baseman and second base is the

_____ .

GO TO PART E IN YOUR TEXTBOOK

A STORY DETAILS

Work the items.

1. When Edward begged at farmhouses, the people ▒▒▒ him.

   a. welcomed   b. ignored

   c. were rude to

2. Edward saw a _____ hanging on an open barn door.

3. Edward decided to enter the barn because it looked ▒▒▒ .

   a. hostile   b. like a hospital

   c. hospitable

4. Two farm ▒▒▒ came into the barn after Edward entered.

   a. hands   b. animals   c. owners

5. Edward went to bed in a ▒▒▒ .

   a. cot   b. barrel   c. stall

6. Edward covered himself with blankets that smelled like _____ .

7. Edward discovered that he was lying next to a _____ .

8. Edward rearranged his bed so he could get ▒▒▒ the animal.

   a. away from   b. next to

   c. on top of

B VOCABULARY

Complete each sentence with the correct word.

brawl	chant	overcast
burly	grope	shattered
calf	hospitable	worm

1. There weren't any shadows on the ground during the _____ day.

2. The family was so _____ that they had guests every night.

3. When the lights went out, we had to _____ our way around the room.

4. The _____ was born in the barn shortly after midnight.

5. The clay pot _____ when it fell off the table onto the tile floor.

6. The basketball fans began to _____ loudly when their team got the ball.

7. Cho had to _____ her way through the crowd of students to get on the bus.

C CHARACTER STATEMENTS

Complete each sentence with *Tom, Edward, Miles, Hugo,* or *Hertford.*

1. _____ said, "I am as comfortable as I was in the palace, even though my bed is only straw."

2. _____ said, "This boy has no talent for begging or stealing."

3. _____ said, "Being a king was hard at first, but I'm getting used to it."

4. _____ said, "I am a knight in the kingdom of dreams."

5. _____ said, "When I return, I will claim my rightful place on the throne."

6. _____ said, "The king seems to be slowly regaining his senses."

GO TO PART D IN YOUR TEXTBOOK

A STORY DETAILS

Work the items.

1. Edward convinced the girls he was the king by telling them ▢ .

   a. about his life in Westminster Palace

   b. he had a crown

   c. he was the king.

2. The girls might not have believed Edward if they had been ▢ .

   a. older   b. younger   c. cousins

3. The girls took Edward to their house when they realized he was

   _____ .

4. The widow thought that Edward was ▢ .

   a. sane   b. crazy   c. handsome

5. What subject did Edward show interest in?

   a. weaving   b. cooking

   c. farming

6. The widow thought that Edward had

   worked in a royal _____ .

7. The widow tested Edward by leaving

   some hot _____ on the stove.

8. What did Edward do with those objects?

   a. nothing   b. ate them

   c. took them off the stove

B VOCABULARY

Complete each sentence with the correct word.

complimented	mooncalf	vagrant
lash	prosper	widow
limb	tragic	

1. A person who does not have any place to live and has no job is a

   _____ .

2. Gamal _____ his opponent for winning the chess game.

3. The soldier's _____ never remarried.

4. It's _____ that so many people are killed in wars.

5. Harry was such a _____ that he wore his clothes backward.

6. Which _____ is more important, an arm or a leg?

7. It's hard to _____ when nobody has any money.

C CHARACTER TRAITS

Complete each sentence with *knows* or *doesn't know*.

1. Edward _____ how to milk a cow.

2. Edward _____ how to fry eggs.

3. Edward _____ how to eat fried eggs.

4. Edward _____ how to give orders.

5. Edward _____ how to shear a sheep.

6. Edward _____ how to plant oats.

D FACT OR FICTION

Write whether each statement is *fact* or *fiction*.

1. There was a king of England named Edward Tudor. _____

2. There was a king of England named Tom Canty. _____

3. There was a king of England named Henry Tudor. _____

4. Some old people are kind to strangers. _____

5. Two old people were turned into trees. _____

GO TO PART D IN YOUR TEXTBOOK

A STORY DETAILS

Work the items.

1. At the beginning of the chapter, Edward ran farther and farther into a

   _____ .

2. Edward saw light coming from a ▨ .

   a. hut   b. barn

   c. lightning bolt

3. A person who lives alone far away from other people is called a

   _____ .

4. The old man claimed that he was a

   _____ .

5. When Edward woke up, he discovered that he was bound and _____ .

6. Which person knocked loudly on the door?

   a. Miles Hendon   b. John Canty

   c. Hugo

7. The old man claimed that he had sent Edward on an _____ .

8. The only sound Edward could make was a ▨ .

   a. yell   b. whisper   c. groan

B VOCABULARY

Complete each sentence with the correct word.

bound	grope	inform
calf	hermit	intends
confess	hospitable	overcast

1. The cow nursed her _____ with milk.

2. The prisoner was dangerous, so he was _____ and gagged.

3. People can _____ themselves by reading books.

4. Someone who lives alone and far from other people is called a

   _____ .

5. Nobody _____ to make mistakes, but they still happen.

6. When people admit they did something, they _____ .

7. When you search blindly with your hands, you _____ .

Complete each sentence with *Edward, Miles,* or *The hermit.*

1. _____ believed he was a wizard.

2. Very few people believed _____ was the king.

3. _____ wanted to get revenge on Henry the Eighth.

4. _____ saved Edward's life by knocking on a door.

Complete each sentence with *Aphrodite, Ares, Hermes, Poseidon,* or *Zeus.*

1. _____ was the chief god.

2. _____ was the messenger god.

3. _____ was the god of the sea.

4. _____ was the god of war.

GO TO PART D IN YOUR TEXTBOOK

A STORY DETAILS

Work the items.

1. Hugo "_____" stepped on Edward's foot to make Edward angry.

2. Edward used a stout _____ to defend himself against Hugo.

3. After the fight, Edward was carried to a _____ of _____ beside the Ruffler.

4. What kind of meat was inside the woman's package?

   a. beef   b. chicken   c. ham

5. The woman thought that _____ had stolen the meat.

6. The man who threatened Edward was a _____ .

7. At first, the police officer led Edward and the others to a ▮▮▮ .

   a. courtroom   b. jail

   c. police station

8. What punishment would Edward have received if the meat was worth more than thirteen pennies?

   a. imprisonment   b. hanging

   c. lashing

B VOCABULARY

Complete each sentence with the correct word.

band	compliment	sentenced
betray	flogged	tragic
capture	innocent	treachery

1. Everyone in the family cried after the _____ death of their dog.

2. The judge _____ the reckless driver to two months in jail.

3. You can _____ a moment in time with a camera.

4. The lawyer argued that her client was _____ of the crime.

5. The farmer was so mad at his tractor that he _____ it with a whip.

6. The _____ of robbers stole almost everything in the village.

7. The innocent boy was a victim of _____ from his own brother.

C | SEQUENCING

Number the following events in the correct sequence.

_____ Edward was sentenced to jail.

_____ Edward and Hugo had a fight.

_____ Miles rescued Edward from the blacksmith.

_____ Edward was accused of being a thief.

_____ Hugo stole a ham from a woman.

D | THEMES

Complete each sentence with the title of a story you have read.

1. "Be kind to strangers" is one theme of

_____ .

2. "Do not trust appearances" is one theme of

_____ .

3. "Love is better than gold" is one theme of

_____ .

E | CLASSIFICATION

Complete each sentence with _wild_ or _domestic_.

1. Rattlesnakes are _____ animals.

2. Poodles are _____ animals.

3. Whales are _____ animals.

4. Giraffes are _____ animals.

5. Goats are _____ animals.

GO TO PART E IN YOUR TEXTBOOK

A STORY DETAILS

Work the items.

1. Miles knew that the police officer had bought the ham for ▓▓ .

    a. a fair price

    b. more than it was worth

    c. less than it was worth

2. The penalty for the police officer's "little joke" was _____ .

3. Edward and Miles journeyed to _____ Hall.

4. Hugh claimed the letter from France said that Miles was _____ .

5. Hugh said that Miles's brother _____ , and also Miles's _____ were dead.

6. Miles planned to marry a woman named _____ .

7. When Miles saw the woman, her face was deathly _____ .

8. Miles believed the letter from France has been written by _____ .

9. After Miles let him go, Hugh ▓▓ a chair.

    a. pulled up

    b. reeled to

    c. jumped into

B VOCABULARY

Complete each sentence with the correct word.

armed	duties	intend
concerns	entry	penalty
confess	inform	reel

1. If you plan to do something, you _____ to do that thing.

2. You should pay attention when something _____ you.

3. After Lin got a jolt of electricity, he began to _____ around the room.

4. The soldier was so heavily _____ that he staggered from the weight.

5. You cannot go out to play until you finish all your household _____ .

6. In basketball, the _____ for a foul is a free throw.

7. The guard stood before the _____ to the castle.

C PROOF

- Miles is having a hard time proving to other people that he really is Miles Hendon.

Complete each sentence with *prove* or *disprove*.

1. If Miles recognizes all the houses in his home village, that might

   _____ that he really is Miles Hendon.

2. If Miles knows exactly how many rooms are in Hendon Hall, that might

   _____ that he really is Miles Hendon.

3. If Hugh does not recognize Miles, that might _____ that Miles really is Miles Hendon.

4. If a letter says that Miles is dead, that might _____ that Miles really is Miles Hendon.

5. If Miles is able to show that Hugh is lying, that might _____ that Miles really is Miles Hendon.

GO TO PART D IN YOUR TEXTBOOK

A STORY DETAILS

Work the items.

1. Edward planned to write a letter to Hertford in English, Latin, and

   _____ .

2. Edith said that Arthur and his father are free from the terror of Hugh because

   they are _____ .

3. In prison, Miles and Edward were tied

   together with _____ .

4. The servant who brought them news in

   prison was named _____
   Andrews.

5. Who had wanted to see Hugh and Edith married before he died?

   a. Arthur   b. Miles's father

   c. Miles

6. What made Edith think that Miles would never return to Hendon Hall?

   a. a letter   b. a rumor

   c. a death certificate

7. Hugh was planning to attend the

   _____ of the new king.

8. For punishment, Miles was put into the

   _____ .

9. At the end of the chapter, Hugh told the guard to ▒▒▒ Edward.

   a. flog   b. stab   c. grab

B VOCABULARY

Complete each sentence with the correct word.

coronation	deny	hesitate
daily	flog	rumor
deathbed	gossip	smuggled

1. There's no time to _____
   when you start running a race.

2. A report that hasn't been confirmed as

   true is called a _____ .

3. A report about other people's private lives

   is called _____ .

4. If you exercise _____ , you
   will get stronger.

5. Thousands of people attended the

   _____ of the new queen.

6. Saleem _____ a candy bar
   into his classroom.

7. Some people think the Earth is flat, and

   they _____ that it's round.

C | CHARACTER TRAITS

**Complete each sentence with *Edward,*
Hugh, Miles, Tom, or *Arthur.***

1. _____ wrote a letter falsely
   claiming that someone had died.

2. Edith had wanted to marry

   _____ , not his brother.

3. _____ wanted to write a
   letter in three languages.

4. People thought that _____
   was the new king.

5. _____ was put in the stocks.

6. _____ ruled Hendon Hall
   after his father died.

GO TO PART E IN YOUR TEXTBOOK

A STORY DETAILS

Work the items.

1. What punishment did Miles take for Edward at the beginning of the chapter?

    a. a tongue-lashing   b. a branding

    c. a flogging

2. After that punishment, Edward used a stick to make Miles an

    _____ .

3. Earlier in the novel, Edward used a sword to make Miles a _____ .

4. The mob on London Bridge was celebrating the _____ of the new king.

5. That event would be held in _____ Abbey.

6. When Tom first saw his mother in the crowd, he _____ to her.

7. What did Tom say to his mother when she ran up to him?

    a. "I'm so happy to see you!"

    b. "What do you want?"

    c. "I don't know you, woman!"

8. How did Tom feel after he said that?

    a. ashamed   b. proud

    c. wronged

B VOCABULARY

Complete each sentence with the correct word.

abbey	hermit	riot
betray	procession	sentence
ceremony	reclaim	treachery

1. Students went to the lost-and-found room to _____ items they had lost.

2. The coronation would be held in the large _____ .

3. Many people were hurt during the wild _____ .

4. The first car in the funeral _____ carried the casket.

5. The judge had to _____ many guilty people to jail.

6. Everyone laughed during the happy wedding _____ .

7. The _____ lived all by herself far from town.

C POINT OF VIEW

Write whether each passage has *first-person*, *second-person*, or *third-person* point of view.

Passage A

The old town didn't look the same. The movie theater had closed down. The train station was boarded up. The water tower was gone.

We couldn't figure out what had happened. We drove around and around, looking for some signs of life. But we didn't see anything moving, not even a bird.

_____

Passage B

The new Ejecto toaster oven is packed with exciting features. You can operate the toaster with a remote control. You can spin your bread while it's toasting to make it light and fluffy. Best of all, you can push the eject button and have the toast land on your plate. You don't even have to open the door!

_____

Passage C

Golden Acres is a typical suburb. It has several big-box stores, and it's close to the freeway. Except for the paint color, it's hard to tell one house from another. They all have three bedrooms, two bathrooms, a living room, a dining room, and a kitchen. There's also a basement, where all the kids go to play. When I'm in the basement with my friends, my mother shuts the door and says, "Don't make too much noise."

_____

GO TO PART D IN YOUR TEXTBOOK

A STORY DETAILS

Work the items.

1. Edward interrupted the coronation just as
   the _____ was lowering the
   crown onto Tom's head.

2. When Hertford looked carefully at the two
   boys, he saw that they were ▨ .
   a. identical   b. brothers
   c. not similar

3. Hertford began to ask Edward some
   _____ to see if he was the
   real king.

4. Hertford asked Edward about an object
   called the royal _____ .

5. Edward said the object was inside a ▨ .
   a. cabinet   b. safe   c. drawer

6. As the lords on the platform waited for
   Lord Saint John, they formed a ring
   around _____ .

7. When Lord Saint John returned he said the
   object was ▨ .
   a. locked up   b. missing
   c. broken

8. After Lord Saint John spoke, Hertford
   threatened to put Edward under
   _____ .

B VOCABULARY

**Complete each sentence with the
correct word.**

archbishop	coronation	platform
arrest	gossip	rumor
bishop	imposter	smuggle

1. Tom looked like a real king, but he was an
   _____ .

2. The _____ was more
   important than the other bishops.

3. They had to delay the
   _____ because nobody
   could find the crown.

4. The president stood on a
   _____ so everyone could
   see her.

5. The police officer caught the thief in the
   store and placed him under
   _____ .

6. The news about a flying horse was just a
   _____ that wasn't true.

7. The gang used a tunnel to
   _____ stolen goods out of
   the country.

C FACT OR FICTION

Write whether each statement is *fact* or *fiction.*

1. Henry Tudor was a king of England.
   _____

2. Tom Canty was a king of England.
   _____

3. A dog named Buck pulled a thousand-pound sled. _____

4. Dogs were used to pull sleds in the Yukon.
   _____

5. A man was able to change objects into gold. _____

6. Some people think that gold is evil.
   _____

D SETTINGS

Complete each sentence with *Canada*, *England*, *Greece*, *Maine*, *North Carolina*, or *Turkey*.

1. _____ is the setting for "Adventure on the Rocky Ridge."

2. _____ is the setting for *The Prince and the Pauper*.

3. _____ is the setting for "For the Love of a Man."

4. _____ is the setting for "A Horse To Remember."

5. _____ is the setting for "Ron's Summer Vacation."

6. _____ is the setting for "The Golden Touch."

7. _____ is the setting for "The Miraculous Pitcher."

GO TO PART D IN YOUR TEXTBOOK

A STORY DETAILS

Work the items.

1. Before Edward remembered where the seal was, he said, "I cannot recall the event, so I cannot ▇▇▇ the throne."

   a. regain   b. remain   c. retain

2. Edward finally remembered that the seal was in the _____ of a suit of armor.

3. Lord _____

   _____ was sent to find the seal.

4. Finding the seal proved that Edward was the real _____ of England.

5. The seal was supposed to be used for making papers ▇▇▇ .

   a. fireproof   b. official   c. void

6. Tom had used the seal for cracking

   _____ .

7. Where was Miles during the coronation ceremony?

   a. in Westminster Abbey

   b. on London Bridge

   c. outside London

8. Miles hoped to see Sir

   _____ Marlow at the palace.

9. The whipping boy was Sir Marlow's

   _____ .

B VOCABULARY

Complete each sentence with the correct word.

crowning	deny	regain
daily	hesitate	threaded
deathbed	occasions	thundered

1. The soccer player _____ her way through the other team's players and shot a goal.

2. The dog escaped on many

   _____ before its guardians fixed the fence.

3. The country changed for the better after the _____ of the new king.

4. Ms. Lopez was on her

   _____ for several days before she passed away.

5. The police helped Parth

   _____ his stolen bicycle.

6. The sound of the electric bass

   _____ inside the concert hall.

7. On a warm, sunny day, nobody can

   _____ that the weather is perfect.

C   TEXT STRUCTURE AND MAIN IDEA

Work the items.

Paragraph A

In the 1500s, rich English sheep farmers started buying up land for their sheep and even stealing land that didn't belong to them. As a result, many poor farmers lost their farms. These poor farmers tried to fight back, and they came up with a famous saying: "Sheep eat men." Sheep don't really eat men, but because of the sheep, many poor farmers were ruined.

1. What main text structure does paragraph A use?

   a. cause and effect

   b. comparison

   c. problem and solution

   d. sequence of events

2. What is the main idea of paragraph A?

   _____

   _____

Paragraph B

Next in power after the Royal Family were the lords and ladies. Some lords and ladies lived in the king's palace. Others had their own castles and controlled large areas of land. The king gave the lords and ladies different titles to show how powerful they were. Duke and duchess were the most powerful titles, followed by marquess and marchioness; earl and countess; viscount and viscountess; and baron and baroness. Each lord and lady had certain powers, but they all obeyed the king.

3. What main text structure does paragraph B use?

   a. cause and effect

   b. comparison

   c. problem and solution

   d. sequence of events

4. What is the main idea of paragraph B?

   _____

   _____

GO TO PART D IN YOUR TEXTBOOK

A STORY DETAILS

Work each item.

1. To test whether he was dreaming, Miles _____ down in front of the king.

2. Which two royal titles had Edward given to Miles?

   a. Duke   b. Marquess   c. Earl

   d. Viscount   e. Baron   f. Knight

3. Miles had tried to impress Edward by showing him _____ Hall.

4. When Miles looked around, he saw Edith and _____ near the back of the throne room.

5. Edward gave Tom the title of King's _____ .

6. Edward also gave a small farm to _____ .

7. While Edward was king, he changed the harsh laws that _____ had made.

8. When he spoke to the lords about those laws, Edward would say, "What do you know about _____ ?"

B VOCABULARY

Complete each sentence with the correct word.

abbey	impressed	reclaimed
await	intelligence	riot
ceremony	procession	strict

1. Soldiers in the army have to follow _____ rules.

2. People sat in the courtroom to _____ the jury's verdict.

3. It's hard to be _____ with a tool that doesn't work.

4. The archbishop walked into the _____ followed by a long line of bishops.

5. All the cars in the funeral _____ were black.

6. There are many ways to measure a person's _____ .

7. Javid went to the police and _____ his stolen computer.

C THEMES

Complete each sentence with *Beauty and the Beast*, *For the Love of a Man*, *The Miraculous Pitcher*, *The Prince and the Pauper*, *The Golden Touch*, or *The Cat that Walked by Himself*.

1. "Common things are more valuable than gold" is one theme of

_____.

2. "You have to see suffering before you can understand what it is" is one theme of

_____.

3. "You should be kind to strangers" is one theme of

_____.

4. "You should not trust appearances" is one theme of

_____.

5. "Love is a powerful force" is one theme of

_____.

GO TO PART D IN YOUR TEXTBOOK

A STORY DETAILS

Work the items.

1. The two brothers in the play are

   _____ and

   _____ .

2. The two friends of the brothers are

   _____ and

   _____ .

3. In Act 1, the backyard is covered in

   _____ from a big storm.

4. When it's under the porch, the dog makes

   a _____ sound.

5. The children go into the house to ask Celia

   Andrews and _____ J if
   they can keep the dog.

6. One of the characters says, "Many

   _____ make light work."

7. When the unusually clever dog gets a
   command, she ▮▮▮ it.

   a. ignores   b. obeys

   c. doesn't understand

8. What does Celia mean when she asks "Who
   knew?" at the end of Act 1, Scene 2?

   a. Which one of the children knew the dog?

   b. Who knew the storm was coming?

   c. Who would have expected the children
      to do all the work?

B VOCABULARY

Complete each sentence with the correct word.

await	intelligence	strict
debris	occasion	vicious
impressed	perplexed	whimper

1. The _____ wildcat chased
   a rabbit across the field.

2. Andrew was _____ by the
   difficult puzzle.

3. The airplane crash left tons of

   _____ across the meadow.

4. The day you graduate from school is an

   important _____ .

5. The monkey had a lot of

   _____ and could add,
   subtract, multiply, and divide.

6. The dog began to _____ by
   the door to go outside.

7. The passengers gathered at the airport to

   _____ their flights.

C THEATER TERMS

Work the items.

1. Plays take place on a
   _____ .

2. Scenes in a play are organized into
   _____ .

3. In printed plays, what do the words in
   italic type show?

   a. actors' lines   b. stage directions

   c. characters' names

4. What do the words in parentheses tell
   characters?

   a. what to say   b. what to ignore

   c. what to do

5. What words appear in CAPITAL
   LETTERS?

   a. actors' lines   b. stage directions

   c. characters' names

GO TO PART E IN YOUR TEXTBOOK

A STORY DETAILS

Work the items.

1. Jacob bought treats for the dog to ▆▆ .
   a. eat while watching TV
   b. use as rewards for learning
   c. feed the dog breakfast

2. The dog was able to ▆▆ all the children's commands.
   a. interrupt   b. integrate
   c. interpret

3. Which character thought the dog was learning way too fast?
   a. Vera   b. Caleb   c. Jacob
   d. Miguel

4. Daniel Cruz interviewed the children in the ▆▆ .
   a. house   b. backyard
   c. front yard

5. When the interview was over, Nell said, "That's a _____ !"

6. The dog's real owner was Ms. _____ .

7. The dog was a ▆▆ actor.
   a. canine   b. feline   c. bovine

8. Teaching tricks to dogs takes a lot of ▆▆ .
   a. repossession   b. repentance
   c. repetition

B VOCABULARY

Complete each sentence with the correct word.

astounded	interpret	regain
crowning	precise	repetition
inquisitive	reconsider	threaded

1. Reporters need to be _____ to get all the details of a story.

2. It was hard to _____ what the baby was trying to say.

3. The new evidence forced the judge to _____ the case.

4. The carpenter took _____ measurements before cutting the wood.

5. All the people were _____ when the goat began to speak English.

6. The key to learning how to play a musical instrument is _____ .

7. The fleet-footed deer _____ its way through the thick woods.

GO TO PART E IN YOUR TEXTBOOK